The Way He Chose

Jennifer Jireh

WESTBOW®
PRESS
A DIVISION OF THOMAS NELSON
& ZONDERVAN

WestBow Press books may be ordered through booksellers or by contacting:

WestBow Press
A Division of Thomas Nelson & Zondervan
1663 Liberty Drive
Bloomington, IN 47403
www.westbowpress.com
1 (866) 928-1240

ISBN: 978-1-4908-5823-4 (sc)
ISBN: 978-1-4908-5824-1 (e)

Library of Congress Control Number: 2014919301

Printed in the United States of America.

WestBow Press rev. date: 12/10/2014

Contents

Dedication

This book is dedicated to the glory of the Lord Jesus Christ who has given my life meaning, to my children, Kim, Paul, Heidi and David who stuck by me and supported me through difficult years and to my grandchildren who bring so much joy into my heart.

Foreword

As a young girl I had a dream, not a night dream but one I built in my heart growing up in a small Texas town. I saw myself in a tidy little country house with lots of happy, noisy children scampering about, a collie dog and a loving husband coming home in the evenings to make the cozy picture complete. It was a simple dream and my young mind never considered that it would not one day come true.

This book tells the story of the way my life really happened, much of it a nightmare, a disastrous marriage, facing death through illness and at the end of a loaded gun, dealing with fear and confusion, loneliness, bitterness and hate, raising my four precious children alone. But the real truth and message of the story is how in the midst of it all I found God to be a reality. When I cried out in desperation he came into my life and gently loved me, healed me and changed me. He took the broken pieces and put them together in a vessel fit for his work, his glory and sent me to Mexico to the mission field. He has done miracles too numerous to count, many of them retold in the pages of this book. He showed me Jesus and filled me with his Spirit. Some of the names I've changed as it is not my intention to judge nor embarrass but the facts are true as I remember them. Much of the ugly and some of the good have not been included for various reasons. It is not the story of a path I would have chosen for me and my children but although much more difficult with many more obstacles, perhaps a better one. It is the way He chose.

1

Lots of Courage or Little Sense

As the rickety old van bumped along the narrow, potholed highway, I found myself wondering if perhaps mother was right. Maybe I had lost all my senses as she so vividly proclaimed to take David away from his friends and school and set out for central Mexico and a whole new lifestyle. David, at fourteen was willing enough. He was always in favor of an adventure and that's how he looked at the change. But try as I might, I couldn't shake the negative attack from my mind. Her words kept piercing my thoughts like little poison, darts. "You are crazy to go to Mexico and take David," she had shouted.

"Mother, we are going to help the people, to do God's work and God will take care of us," I replied, knowing it was useless to try to explain.

"Well, I still say you'll get you both killed or starve to death. You better stay home where you belong!"

Boy, did she ever know how to get to me. I had long ago come to understand that my mother would never accept the radical changes in my life since I had surrendered it 100% to God in 1972. The fact that I was forty didn't matter nor that I had managed to raise my four children alone, halfway across the nation from her watchful eye. At least David was almost grown and he was the youngest. But Mother always knew what was best for me and made no bones about trying to make me see that I had gone off the deep end with this new religion as she called it. Usually, when I was out of earshot my confidence would return but today was different. The decision to move to Tampico hadn't come easy for me and her words had cut deep into the wisdom behind that decision.

David shifted his position slightly as the wheel of the van hit a large pothole causing a jolt. It was impossible to miss them all. He lay slouched back against the seat, his Indiana Jones hat pulled down over his eyes, trying to nap. The old felt hat had once belonged to my dad. David had steamed it, reshaped the brim and added a band of rattlesnake hide that he and his brother, Paul, had skinned out and preserved from a big, Texas rattler. If he had any qualms about the move, they were well hidden. So as we continued to jostle along toward our new home, I was left alone with my thoughts. The long hassle at the border had eaten away much of our day so I pressed a bit harder on the accelerator. Barring any trouble we would make Tampico before sundown. The thought of being on this isolated road after dark didn't appeal to me in the least. Besides, if we were attacked or killed by outlaws my mother could say "I told you so."

Our old International Travel-all was packed to the hilt. Some of it was housekeeping supplies, some personal things and some food and clothing for the poor around Tampico. At the border after unpacking and repacking I had to pay a guard $10 to get us on the road again. Using those wooden ammunition crates I had picked up at the Army surplus store had definitely been a mistake. Naturally they were packed in the bottom of the van and the guards wanted to see inside them.

"How much farther now?" David asked, as he lifted the brim of his hat for a look around.

"I'm not sure. Why don't you check the map?" I replied. After studying the map briefly, David noted that Ciudad Victoria was next on our route and Tampico should be about three more hours down the road. Folding the map haphazardly, he shoved it on to the dash, then, as if reading my mind, he looked over at me and said," Don't worry Mom. It'll work out for us."

Knowing that David was relaxed helped me to loosen up a bit. He was right of course. Things had always worked out for us. Troubles seemed to follow me around like fleas on a hound dog but somehow things always worked out. Over and over again, God had proved to me that whenever I encountered trouble, he was always there with a way out if I kept my head enough to look for his leading. That seemed to be the hard part. My life had been a lot like a jungle maze and behind every tree lurked a new danger, a new challenge to my wits. But from the many tough experiences, I had learned a lot about faith. God had shown me that faith and fear are exact opposites and one cancels out the other. Sadly enough, I had never learned to trust God until I was past thirty. I grew up believing in God. At church we sang about trust, the preacher preached about trust but I never saw a lot of it in action when it got right down to it.

As my mind wandered back over the years I realized how different my life had been to what I had always dreamed about as a young girl growing up. During the very early years of my life the family moved around a lot but we settled on a small farm in north central Texas when I was twelve and stayed in the area until I graduated from high school. I had breezed through school keeping an "A" average with very little effort. School work just always came easy for me. Many of my teachers encouraged me to go to college after high school. I even decided to make college plans when a wealthy aunt offered to pay my tuition to Abilene Christian College. But secretly all I ever really wanted was a home, a loving husband, lots of children, a flower garden and a quiet life.

There were seven children in my family and I was number six. My oldest sister, Wanda, was married before I was born and my parents were more like grandparents than a mother and father to me. Six years before I came along, my dad had a nervous breakdown. He lost his health and the family business. After that we were always poor but as I remember it we didn't have such a bad life. We wore some hand-me-down clothing, raised our own chickens and grew most of our vegetables on our rented farm. Mother was good at managing Dad's partial disability check from an old WW1 injury and Dad worked odd jobs occasionally. Dad was red headed, of Scotch Irish descent and witty with a sense of humor. Mother was dark-haired, mostly English descent, and nearly always serious. I grew up with my older sister Bobbie and my younger sister Kay. Wanda had died tragically of cancer when I was nine, leaving behind a husband and four-year-old son, Ronnie. My brother, Kenneth, was killed in an auto accident on Christmas eve when I was ten, the victim of a drunk driver. My brother, T. W. and sister, Bettie, were grown and living away from home. Bobbie and Kay were close and did all the young girl things together but for the most part, I was a loner, a thinker and a dreamer. Being overly sensitive, I remember crying at the drop of a hat. Since people often said and did things that hurt my feelings, it made sense to me to stay away from them as much as possible and so I did. My favorite pastime was walking around the farm with my collie dog or climbing into the hayloft with a good book. I can still remember the fresh smell of the newly plowed earth, while walking down the rows of corn in the spring.

Much of our time growing up was spent on chores. We tended the vegetable garden, hoed the long rows of corn, did the laundry in an old, wringer type washer and hung it on the line to dry, carried in wood and kindling for the fireplace in winter and milked our Jersey cow. Our old cow, Bessie, as opposed to most, would let you milk from either side so two of us would get on opposite sides, turn an old bucket upside down for a stool and begin the chore. Quite often, the temptation to squirt a partner was irresistible and we wasted some of the milk. It usually meant trouble with mother when our milk quota came up short. We used an outdoor privy and drew our water from a well until we moved into town my sophomore year of high school. In town I took a waitress job in a small café evenings and Saturdays to make money for school needs.

Our little town of Graford, didn't have a movie theater, so on New Year's Eve of my senior year, I went with a girlfriend to the movies in the neighboring town of Mineral Wells. There she introduced me to Joe, a soldier from the local Fort Wolters air base. His hair was as black as his leather jacket and he was obviously older. When he showed an interest in me that evening I was impressed. Joe soon became a regular visitor at our house and no one seemed to mind that he was almost eleven years my senior. In April when he asked me to marry him I said yes and canceled my college plans. Joe was possessive and moody at times but being in love can make you do dumb things and I chose to ignore his bad side. He also said he drank beer, but knowing I disapproved of it, he never drank around me and said he would quit altogether. I was naïve enough to believe him. Two weeks after my graduation we were married in a small ceremony at the Protestant chapel on base.

What followed was thirteen years of agony as I remember it. His heavy drinking, the other women, the physical and mental abuse, running and hiding with the children, afraid for our safety, our lives, the crying, the pain, his promises to change, my confusion, my hope that things would be different though they never were, my love for him that didn't want to die! Finally when I knew it was get out or crack into a million pieces, I moved into a mobile home we had on some land north of town and filed for divorce. At times, when Joe was drunk he said he would kill me if I ever divorced him. At that point I figured some things are worse than dying and the way we were living was one of those things. I'm sure that in all those years there must have been some good times but the only ones I remember are the good times I had with my children. God gave me four beautiful and gifted children. I adored them from the moment I knew they were growing inside of me. I treasured the role of being a mother and tried to cover the children with a blanket of love and affection to make up for the almost constant climate of fear and confusion in which they lived. When they started school, I made sure they were dressed neatly and checked on their homework. I attended their school programs and little league ball games. I made them costumes for special events and did everything I knew in an effort to make their lives as normal and happy as possible.

The festering sore we called a marriage, erupted one horror filled night when Joe came to the mobile home drunk, held a loaded gun and described how he was going to kill me and the children and maybe himself. He had not decided that yet. He first, forced me outside to watch as he began breaking the windows out of my car with the butt of the rifle but he made a mistake and his arm went through one of the windows causing a jagged sliver of glass to cut a major vessel in his wrist. Cursing, he laid the rifle on top of the car, pulled me back inside the house and ordered me to fix it. The blood ran down my bathrobe and splattered on the walls, the table and the floor.

When Joe had first sat in the living room chair and casually loaded the gun and the nightmare began, I tried to think of a way to get the children out alive. They were in their beds asleep except for Kim who awakened and cried out "Daddy, please don't kill Mommy". When he told her to shut up she got quiet. I wracked my brain but there was no way, so silently I prayed. "God help us, please help us." Over and over I pleaded to God for help. The praying seem to keep me from cracking under the pressure that my mind didn't know how to handle. I wrapped his wrist in strips of cloth I cut from a tee-shirt. After about an hour of walking the floor, cursing and threatening, he passed out from the liquor and loss of blood. Quickly, I took the children and we slipped away. God spared our lives that night and I will forever be grateful that he answered my cry for help when there was no way we could help ourselves.

We hid out at my sister's lake cabin and as always, Joe began to call my family and try to find me. I wasn't willing to risk the lives of the children again so I sent word he would never see them unless he checked into the psychiatric ward of the Veteran's Hospital in Dallas. He agreed to go if I would drive him over. I knew it might be a trick to get me alone but at least the children would be safe, so I agreed to take him. After notifying the hospital we would be coming, I picked him up and we headed for Dallas. I was rigid with fear the entire trip and didn't relax until we walked through the automatic doors of the hospital. There, I spent the day answering the doctors questions. They kept Joe for three months. I visited him once a week and while he was there on medication, he seemed calm and in control. The doctors gave me technical names for his condition and some of the reasons for his behavior but admitted they did not know the real cause. At the end of three months, Joe was allowed a weekend pass and came to the place in the country where the kids and I were living. On Monday he refused to return to the hospital and threw away his medicine, saying he didn't need it. That's when I decided to go far away and start a new life for the safety and sanity of the kids and myself. I knew if we stayed, the same thing could happen again and next time we might not get away. Every ounce of hope that we could ever make it together finally died. I had nothing left in me to try.

A friend from church had mentioned vacationing at a town in Florida. It was on the Gulf and large enough to find a good job. I was desperate and that was the only place I could think of, so Pensacola, Florida became our destination. The following Saturday morning, after Joe left for town, I hurriedly packed the station wagon with some of our things. I told the kids that Daddy was going to be sick again because he threw away his medicine and we had to leave. Except for David, who was only three, they knew exactly what I meant and helped me pack and load. Kim was nine, Paul was eight and Heidi was six. Sadly, we took their Shetland pony to a neighbor boy and loaded in the station wagon. As we left town, headed down the road to a place we had never been, with a few personal items and $250 I had borrowed from my folks, I was scared senseless of what lay ahead but was more afraid of what was behind, so I kept going down that road. Ever since I was a young girl I have loved to sing. A hymn came to me and as I sang, the kids joined in. It seemed to calm my jagged nerves as we kept going down that lonely road.

"Hey, Mom, the gas is getting low," David said, pointing at the gas gauge and jolting me back to the present.

"Yeah, I see. We'll stop at the next town and fill up. That should get us to Tampico." It was July and the hot, desert air blasted in the window, blowing strands of my unruly hair across my face. The desert had a lonely feeling in spite of its rugged beauty. The purple sage bushes were in full bloom, as were they saguaro cactus that seemed to be reaching for the sky with their long arms shooting in the air. The highway was virtually deserted and at times, ten minutes would pass before we would see another vehicle. I looked over at David who had retreated beneath his hat again. He was not a model teenager. He nearly always argued or complained when I asked or told him to do something. He avoided physical labor like the plague unless it was something he wanted to do and he rarely changed his socks unless I insisted. In short, he was a bit rebellious and a bit lazy but I saw in David two qualities that overshadowed his shortcomings. I saw his compassion and faith in God. He was always doctoring sick or injured animals. Several months back on his first mission trip across the border we went to San Francisco, Coahuila and witnessed some pitiful sights. One was a family of nine, living in a two room, dirt floor hut. The poppa smelled of liquor and squatted outside the hacienda with his bottle. The baby was sick and the three year old girl sat in the dirt, eating her plate of black beans while laying her tortilla on the ground beside her. When we left the place, David couldn't hold back the tears. Wiping them away with the back of his hand he said," Mom, how can we help them? We have to help them!"

So I had witnessed David's compassionate side and knew his faith in God was strong and healthy. All of the children had seen miracles that no amount of science, technology or knowledge could explain away. Like the time I let our toy terrier, Celia, outside our Arlington apartment to tend to business. She barked at a German shepherd in our yard and he took one bite. His teeth pierced her tiny spinal cord and from all indications, she began to die. Her head drew backwards and her eyeballs rolled up, almost out of sight. Her little legs stiffened and paralyzed and she lost control of her bladder and bowel. If I was a gambler, I wouldn't have given her one chance in a million to live. The children began to cry and I felt heartbroken and utterly helpless. Then a strange thing happened. As we gently lifted her onto a board and carried her inside, I heard a voice inside me say;" I will heal her if you pray."

"But she's dying," I argued. Once again the voice repeated the message. I thought about what the children would think if I told them the dog would get well and then she died. I waited but the voice did not return. After tossing it around for a minute or so, I told the kids we were going to pray for the dog and God would heal her. There, I had done it but I still believed she was going to die! To make matters worse, the children believed me. They were smiling and excited. What had I done? It was too late to back down now so we gathered around our dead looking dog, held hands and asked God to heal her. When the accident happened, we were packed and ready to go to my folk's farm at Lone Camp, about two hours away to spend the night. So I put Celia in the utility room still looking like she was dead. I put down papers and fresh food and water near her head, in the unlikely event that she might need them." Dummy", I thought." This dog will be dead when we return." But when the kids expressed concern about leaving her, I assured them she would be okay. All week-end I kept thinking about what I would tell them when we found the dog dead.

On Sunday afternoon, we went home. The kids ran ahead to the utility room and I was feeling like a traitor. When they opened the door and Celia walked out, I almost fainted from shock and relief. She walked a little crooked and a little slow but she was alive and walking. So it had been God's voice after all, and he had healed her. Within a few days, Celia was completely normal and we all got a major lesson in faith.

I thought about how I had not always been the perfect mother that I set out to be but since 1972, I had sought to find and follow God. I always tried to discern his voice and study his word and no matter how ridiculous it looked or seemed, if I thought it was God, I did it. I had been wrong a few times but I had been right a lot more, and the faith that I had learned to live by had gotten down inside all my children and I knew it was there to stay.

2

Hard Times and Hermit Crabs

Speeding along toward Tampico that hot afternoon, I began to wonder what had brought me to this place in my life. Less than ten years ago I had been living a more or less self-centered life in northern Florida. Now, here I was, headed into the heart of Mexico to find an orphanage that I felt God had told me about. Back in Florida, we had a four bedroom, three bath townhouse that I had furnished like the cover of a GOOD HOUSEKEEPING magazine. I drove a new car and had a good job with a substantial raise every six months. I liked to entertain and threw occasional parties for my friends. Two evenings each week I went to college to study art and English. I sailed, played tennis and golf, attended Community Theater regularly and dated a number of men. I was doing just about everything I wanted to do. What had brought me from what I wanted in my life to what God wanted? The answer had to be God and my unconditional surrender to his will. Nothing or no one else could have made such a drastic change in me.

As David napped, my thoughts went back to our first few months in Pensacola. They were difficult in many respects. For $100 a month, we rented a small cottage within walking distance of the bay. The location proved to be a good choice as the kids and I needed a release after the years of tension. The water and the beach provided one. My nerves were raw and I jumped at every loud noise. At moments I could relax and enjoy the children or the sun and the beach, but without warning, the old tensions and fears would return and the pit of my stomach would contract.

I wondered if Joe would carry out his threats and if I could make a living for the children and myself. Even though I had several years experience of mechanical drafting design, so far I hadn't been able to find a good job in Pensacola. I always liked art and drawing so I studied it in high school and took private lessons from a professional artist when I had the $10 to pay for them. After I married, Joe could never decide if he wanted me to work or stay home. He kept telling me to get a job and after a few weeks or months he would make me quit. Once, when he told me to get a job I convinced an oil equipment company, Perry Equipment, in Mineral Wells to hire me as a drafting trainee. From that beginning, I had worked my way up to designing machinery. I had to change jobs a lot but tried always to be a hard working, conscientious, employee so my bosses always gave me good recommendations, making it easier to land another job. In Pensacola, I settled temporarily for some odd jobs through Manpower and cleaned house for the elderly couple next door. Kim did some babysitting when I was home to help and Paul mowed lawns. We barely scraped by.

The kids couldn't have been more helpful. They had all brought piggy banks from Texas and when I had no money they were more than willing to donate theirs. Kim had half dollars, Paul, quarters, Heidi, nickels and dimes and David, pennies. We had used them all at different times except the pennies. One Saturday the kids helped me wrap the pennies in coin wrappers and I put them in my purse to buy milk, bread and peanut butter on Monday. On Sunday we went to church as usual. I had always believed in God but didn't know him as a loving father, much less Lord. I just believed he was somewhere up in heaven and I always sought his help when I had a serious problem. Like the time when David was born and everything that could go wrong, did. He came seven weeks early by caesarean section. I had a rare condition, placenta privia, where the afterbirth got below the baby and blocked the birth canal. In the hospital, I was plagued with severe kidney infection and finally, peritonitis (gangrene) when a nurse failed to administer penicillin regularly as the doctor had ordered.

David weighed only three pounds, fourteen ounces and his lungs were not completely developed. He lost down to an even three pounds and was critical from birth until he was several weeks old. The family was called in to say goodbye to me when the doctor said there was no hope. No one ever told me that I was not expected to live but I got the idea from all the weeping friends and family. I only knew that the pain I felt in my abdomen was like none I had ever experienced in my twenty-seven years. I got a morphine shot about every four hours but it only stopped the pain for about one hour, so I was almost constantly in terrible pain. The fever of over 100° had plagued me for weeks. I had a catheter, a stomach pump and an IV needle that had to be changed daily because of collapsing veins.

At one point it was in my foot. I was too weak to speak above a whisper and the nurses had to turn me from side to side with a sheet because I was unable to turn myself over in the bed. At times, I wanted to just die and escape the misery. None of the older children or David had been allowed in my room because the cause of the fever was still unknown. The doctor didn't want to expose the children in the event I had something contagious.

One morning, when the nurses appeared at the door with all four of my children, I knew they had brought them to say goodbye. As they stood at my bedside looking so sad and confused, it broke my heart. I got to see my new baby that a nurse held in one hand. I realized I couldn't die. They needed me! When they were gone and I was alone, I cried and silently begged God to spare my life. I desperately wanted to live for the sake of my children and God was my only hope. I asked for just five more years. I told him that nobody would love my children like I did and I would take them to church and teach them about Jesus. He must have listened, because a specialist was called in from Fort Worth to do surgery and to everyone's amazement, I survived. After forty-two days I went home from the hospital. David came home two weeks later. I remember the morning I was dismissed; the doctor put me into a wheelchair and wheeled me out onto a small veranda. The grass and sky had never looked more beautiful.

"Well, Jen," he said," tell me, what does heaven look like?"

"What do you mean?" I asked, confused.

"You got as close as any human can without crossing over, he replied, "and I thought you might have gotten a glimpse." I don't know, Doctor Hamilton, I responded. "If I saw it, I don't remember but I can tell you about the other place because I've been there."

"Yes, I guess you have," he said quietly and pushed me back inside.

I kept my promise to God and took the kids to church regularly. That particular Sunday that I had the rolled pennies in my purse, a visiting missionary was speaking. She told of the great things God was doing in South America and spoke of the need to get the gospel and food and clothing to the poor natives there. Earlier, the preacher had announced that the collection that Sunday would go for the work in South America. When the plate was passed, Heidi bent over and whispered," Mom can we give our pennies to those poor people?" I hesitated. Right now we were poor people and those pennies were all we had for food! At that moment, a scripture popped into my head, Luke 6:38, "Give and it shall be given unto you---"

"If the others agree we will give our pennies," I answered, secretly hoping there would be a dissenter in the group. To my dismay, the other children agreed and I was thinking that scripture better work in a hurry as the kids dropped in our last six dollars in the world. The next morning, a letter came in the mail from Mother with a check inside. It was $200. I had left some furniture behind for her to sell if she could find a buyer and she had sold it. The kids and I rejoiced. We celebrated by going to McDonalds for hamburgers and shakes that evening. God had come through with perfect timing and we learned a valuable lesson about giving.

One Saturday morning, when I answered a knock at the door, there stood Joe. Instinctively, like a lioness who knows when her cubs are threatened, I sensed danger. "What do you want?" I asked coldly.

"I just came to check on the kids," he replied.

"They are just fine," I said.

"Well, I'll just see for myself," he said as he opened the screen door, pushed me aside and walked in.

Friends often asked why I never called the police for protection. The reason was that I knew if I ever had him arrested, that when he was released, he would find us and we would pay. When the children saw Joe, except for David, they were all afraid to approach him. Tension filled the room. Joe bent over and picked up David, then said he had brought the boat and was going to take the kids out in the Gulf.

"I don't think that's a good idea," I replied, feeling that if he took the children I might never see them again. One of Joe's favorite threats had been that he would take the kids and I would never see them again.

"Well, you can come along or stay but I'm taking the kids." Carrying David, he headed out the door and told the other children to get into his pickup truck. Knowing he would use force if necessary and he already had David, I told the children to go to the truck and following them, I climbed into the crowded cab. I could feel my body tremble as I held Heidi tightly in my lap. Kim sat next to Joe, holding David and Paul sat between Kim and me. It seemed as if we would never be free from the fear and threats that he held over our heads. I thought how terrible it must be for the children to fear harm from their own father.

As Joe launched the eighteen foot boat, I noticed the wind warning flags were flying.

"We can't take the kids out," I shouted." The wind warning flags are up. See?" I said pointing.

"Nah," was his only reply. Joe put David in the boat. Shaking, I helped Heidi aboard while Kim and Paul climbed in unaided. As we made our way out into the channel, we met a line of vessels coming into shore. Joe ignored them. Our boat crashed around crazily, like a toy, in the raging waves. I begged Joe to turn around. He just smiled, not saying anything and kept going. I thought, dear God, it's going to be a replay of the night in Mineral Wells and fought the rising panic in my throat. I put the children in the space beneath the bow but when the boat came crashing down off the giant waves at full speed, they banged their heads and Heidi and David began to cry. As I tried to quiet and comfort them, I knew once again, God was our only hope. Silently, I began to pray that he would somehow save us.

By the time we reached the three mile buoy marker, the waves were even bigger and the wind, stronger. The buoy clanged wildly as it bounced about in the churning water. There was a continuous stream of craft heading in, including large yachts and shrimp boats. Many of them blasted their horns and motioned for us to turn around. Joe continued to smile and kept going. I knew I had to do something quick. We were sure to swamp and drown in our small boat if we went any farther. I decided to challenge Joe, something I had rarely done in our thirteen year marriage. Like my father, I had always been a peacemaker and would usually go to any length to let Joe have his way or try to keep him calm to avoid a fight. When things got unbearable I would take the children and slip away. We left home over a dozen times and always Joe would find us. Sometimes, he would say he was sorry and beg us to come home. Other times, he would threaten or force us. It is hard to explain why I stayed thirteen years. The first few years I still loved him and hoped desperately that things would change. Also, I had been taught that marriage is forever and divorce was comparable to the unforgivable sin. I was bothered too, by the question of forgiveness. If someone asked you to forgive them, didn't that mean you were to forgive and try to forget? Later I was able to see things quite differently, but then I was young and confused.

"We're going back," I shouted as I stood up and grabbed the wheel in an effort to turn the boat around. Just then a large wave crashed over the side, setting the boat on edge. We took in a lot of water and straightened up just in time for a second wave to hit, this time, from behind. I was still holding the wheel. Looking at Joe, I could see he was deciding what to do. After a moment or two, he released the wheel, leaned back in the seat and laughed. When I got the boat headed back toward shore, I pressed the automatic pump button to remove the water we had taken in. The kids and I were shaken and bruised. They were crying. We might not make it back to shore alive and Joe was laughing. I wondered what could ever cause a man, who should normally love and protect his family, to delight in their suffering and deliberately risk their lives. It was beyond my understanding. We made it back to shore safely and went home. Joe had had his fun and left that afternoon. I thanked God for sparing our lives one more time.

It was several weeks before we recovered from the boat experience but slowly we relaxed and began to live our normal lives again. The kids' school grades all began to improve. Paul's last year of school in Mineral Wells had been a real trial. His teacher regularly complained about his daydreaming, unfinished work and detached attitude. In Pensacola, he took an almost immediate interest in school work and activities and never made below a "B" average again. David was too young for school but definitely had a knack for keeping things lively around the house. Once, when I was working, and he was home with the sitter, he discovered it was fun to run and jump into a large pile of leaves we had raked up in the backyard. When the other kids came home from school, he convinced Paul and Kim to swing him by his arms and legs then toss him into the pile of leaves. On one such toss, his head found the corner of the patio and the resulting cut required several stitches. When the doctor asked David how it happened, he said he ran into an elephant!

Life at our house was sometimes loud, sometimes happy, some rare times quiet, but never, never dull. One morning I woke and thought I saw something moving on the foot of the bedspread. Morning is not my best time so I shook my sleepy head and looked again, hoping I was mistaken. Sure enough, there were several somethings on my spread. I yelled for the kids and they came running. The day before, Kim and Paul had brought me a bowl of pretty shells from the bay and set them on my dresser. It just so happened there were hermit crabs living inside those pretty shells and during the night, they had crawled out and around the room, some of them finding their way onto my bed. The kids thought it was really funny and had a good laugh.

Our new found freedom from constant fear and tension was wonderful but proved a difficult adjustment for me. I kept looking over my shoulder, watching and waiting for the next attack. Although our financial situation was extremely tight I tried to make our first summer there as happy as I could for the kids. We had a tent and went camping at Fort Pickens on the Gulf nearby. We went hiking and exploring along the numerous, nature trails. Rather than pushing the children to make good grades in school I tried to stir up in them an excitement about learning. I taught them to be curious about the wonders of nature and world around them and to look for answers. Being a lover of the natural things God gave us, the trees and woods, the beaches and oceans, the wildflowers, the mountains and birds and butterflies and all the little critters that are out there, I taught them to respect these gifts and to never litter or destroy them.

We watched the tiny shellfish wash ashore with the waves, burrow quickly in the sand and wait for another wave to wash them back out to sea. We studied the funny little sand crabs, with their curious eyes and long legs, skitter about, digging holes that were soon washed away by the tide. If the crabs got discouraged, it never showed. Eagerly and patiently, they would dig another hole. We discovered with wonder, tiny, phosphorescent, microscopic animals that would light up around our feet when we walked along the beach at night, very near the water. We went fishing and caught white bass and pompano. Paul would clean them and Kim would help me cook them for dinner. In the woods, we would sit silently and listen for the different sounds and try to identify them. We poked in logs and under rocks. So, despite our circumstances, our first summer on our own was filled with lots of happy times, times of sharing and learning.

One day I saw an ad in the Pensacola Sunday classified, for a drafting specialist, at Armstrong Cork Company. I decided to go in and apply the following day. I knew the competition would be tough because good jobs were very scarce there. I think it was because lots of people like to live near the beach and Pensacola is on the Gulf of Mexico and has beautiful, white beaches, white because they are chiefly quartz. After I filled out the application on Monday, I was asked to take some tests. After the interview and testing, the project engineer showed me around the large plant that made ceiling tile. It employed about three hundred people. I felt I needed that job and told God so that night.

I didn't hear anything for several days and then the project engineer called. He said that I had done better on the tests than all other applicants but the powers who hired, were against hiring a woman for the job. They argued that I would be working with various plant department heads and bosses who were all men. And they might not take to working on machine design with a woman. He said he was pulling for me and had taken a copy of the company manual to them and read the part about equal opportunity employment. I thanked him for his support and hung up the phone to wait some more. It was three weeks before they decided to hire me. I was the first woman that ever held that position at the plant. I knew I would have to stay on my toes to avoid stupid mistakes and become the brunt of the plant jokes. And I did just that. I double and sometimes triple checked my work. Only one very insecure, little man who was head of the machine shop refused to accept me on the quality of my work and let me know, in no uncertain terms, that I was out of place. I avoided him at times, ignored him at others and stood my ground when I had to.

With the new job, life became easier for the kids and myself. It meant eating out occasionally and a movie now and then. It also meant the new shoes and clothes and other little things that we had been doing without. It looked as if it was going to work. We were in a new place getting our lives together and now I had landed a good job. I remembered to thank God.

3

God Are You Really There?

Although things around me were consistently improving, things inside me were not. In fact, they were quite the opposite. The stress from the past thirteen years which I had kept bottled up tightly inside of me, along with the pressures of coping as a single parent of four young children, began to demand attention. I began to resent and at times, hate Joe, for his failure to provide a home for us. I hated him for the fear and tension we had lived in for so long. When I saw other families out with their dads, little boys fishing with their dads, little girls sitting on daddy's lap or husbands taking their wives to church, picnics or shopping, I hated Joe. He had never been a husband and father to us and he had cruelly destroyed my dream and I hated him for it all. At night, alone in my room I would cry when I thought of the questions that David kept asking." Mommy, why don't we have a daddy who lives with us like Joey?" Or," Mommy, will we ever have another daddy?" The more I remembered, the more the hate, like a cancer, began to eat away my insides, my mind, body and spirit.

In September, I began a required philosophy course at the college. Although I had no way of foreseeing it at the time, that course was to be a spark which ignited a fire and eventually, came within a hairs breadth of destroying me. As we got into the heart of the course, I learned that many of the ancient and great philosophers did not believe in a God, a supreme being, a creator. These educated men had different theories of how the world and man had come into being and what the earth and planets were made of. None of their theories could be proved and they varied as much as night from day. Two of them rarely agreed but it made me begin to question my own beliefs. I think everybody should know and test and prove why and what they believe but my vulnerability to the confusion, resentment and hate, mixed with the idea that God might not exist, catapulted me to the brink of destruction.

I asked myself, didn't I believe in God because I had been taught that he existed? How could I be sure? I believed that the Bible was God's word and that Jesus was his son who died for mankind on the cross, because I had been taught that was truth. But, was it really truth? Why had I been born or anyone for that matter? Maybe all those times I had asked for help and thought God answered, maybe they were just coincidences. If there was a God, why had he allowed my life to get into such a mess? Couldn't he have prevented it somehow? The more I thought about it, the more I became convinced that it was possible that God did not exist. If he did, I could find no evidence of him in my life anymore.

To the resentment, hatred and bitterness were added more confusion, loneliness and depression. I continued to function, go to work, tend the children and take them to church. I had made a promise and on the slim chance that God existed, I was not going back on my word. But inside, I was tormented and barely able to keep from cracking apart at the seams. I tried to think of someone to talk to about the turmoil but I hadn't made any close friends, only casual ones. My children, job, studies and lately, internal problems had occupied all my time. And too, growing up I had been taught that you handle your own problems. I never once remember my parents going to anybody for help of any kind. Perhaps it was a matter of too much pride but that is just the way they were.

As the weeks and months went by and the inner turmoil continued to grow, I finally decided to try to talk to the pastor of our church. When we met in his office, I tried to explain some of the thoughts and feelings that were tormenting me. He listened quietly, then rising from his chair, told me not to worry. Things were sometimes rough in this life but they would get better. I left, feeling more depressed than ever. He did not understand. I could not go on in the condition I was in, without relief, without answers. I felt like a powder keg that was about to explode any minute. A pat on the hand and an encouraging word was like putting a cup of water on a forest fire. It wouldn't work!

After that meeting, I felt there was no more hope. I could no longer cope. I had been going about as a robot, unable to be a real mother to my children. They deserved better. Since I could see no end to my despair and no way out, I considered suicide. I knew my folks would raise the children on their small farm in Texas. I could find out once and for all if there was a God, a heaven or a hell. Thinking about it all I went to my bedroom and locked the door.

"God, if you're there," I said," Jesus, if you are real and have any power to help people, then you have two weeks to show me. Prove to me that you're real and have an answer to my problems because I can't stand the pain anymore. If you don't answer in two weeks, I'm driving my car off the cliff over Escambia Bay."

At one time back in Texas, I had worked at a home for displaced and unwanted children. Parents who couldn't, or didn't want to keep their children, put the kids in the home, where they lived in individual houses with house parents. There were about twelve boys or girls living in each house. Joe was in the Veterans hospital and I worked at the children's home as a weekend house parent. The regular house parents would get an occasional weekend off and I would move in, taking my four children with me. It was difficult and a challenge to mother and manage twelve boys or girls, six to eighteen years of age, as well as my own, but I soon learned that I had a tender heart for those troubled and rejected youngsters. They found it easy to open up to me and soon began to share their problems and feelings. When I arrived in Pensacola, I told the pastor of the church we attended that I would be available to work with troubled youth, if the need ever arose.

The Sunday, after I considered ending my life, after church, a man who seemed to be about my age, approached me and offered his hand.

"I'm Bill Richland," he said," and I hear you might want to work with troubled youngsters." I had forgotten about the offer which I made almost a year earlier and for a moment, stared at him blankly until I remembered.

"Oh, yes," I replied." I did mention that to the pastor when I first came here."

"That's what he said and I might have something going in that direction," Bill remarked. Briefly he explained he was a prosecuting attorney and was bothered by the constant cycle of watching a lot of young kids go to jail, get out, get in trouble and go back to jail. He had been working on a plan that he believed would help them.

"We are having a meeting Thursday night at my house for people who might like to get involved. Could you come?"

"Sure, why not?" I answered thinking to myself I had two more Thursdays. Why not?

On Thursday evening, I had trouble locating the street where Bill lived and arrived several minutes late. I was wondering if I shouldn't have stayed home with the kids when Bill answered the doorbell. He smiled and seemed pleased that I had made it to the meeting. I followed him through the living room to the back of the house, into a large den. When I walked into that room something happened that changed my life. I felt what seemed to be a liquid peace, saturate my body and mind. I had never experienced anything like it in my life. It consumed me. Every care inside of me dissipated and was replaced with love, joy and beautiful peace.

Bill introduced me to his wife and this strange group of people, about twelve in all who were seated in a circle around the room, many on the floor. A couple of them had guitars. Three or four were obvious hippie types and some of the others, I recognized from church. They made a place for me to sit on the floor and then I noticed they all had Bibles. That surprised me. People from our church rarely carried Bibles anywhere except sometimes, to church. They began to sing after Bill led a prayer. Some of the songs I recognized as scripture from the Psalms. The two with guitars played softly. This startled me for a moment. Bill and I and some of the others were members of a church that allowed no musical accompaniment. But I found this warm feeling of peace made it impossible to worry about anything for long. I knew, without a doubt, that what I had encountered in this ordinary room was the presence of God Almighty. He was real after all. It was obvious these people could feel his presence too. Their faces literally glowed as we sang and read scripture and prayed. How odd, I thought, that all my life I had been in church buildings, almost every Sunday, but there in that room, I found for the first time, the presence, the spirit of God. He wasn't just in heaven. He was in that room and in those people.

Later, over refreshments, Bill discussed his twofold plan. He had gotten a judge to agree to place some young offenders in Christian homes instead of jail if Bill could find volunteers. Secondly, he wanted to acquire a sort of halfway house for boys who were getting saved from a street ministry but had no place to live. He thought it was important to get them off the street and grounded in the Word of God before they got into serious trouble themselves. Bill's father was an elder at the church we attended and Bill was trying to get him to purchase a house for this purpose. We all agreed that it sounded like a good idea and I found myself looking forward to the next Thursday!

I drove home that night a different person. The depression and confusion that almost ended my life had vanished. I had my answer. God was very real. He had healed my mind and saved my life one more time. To this day, I have never again doubted the reality of God or his word.

4

He Left Footprints

After God had turned my life around that night at Bill's house, I developed an insatiable hunger to learn more. The Bible became my almost, constant companion. I took a paperback copy to work with me and read it during my lunch hour. I was particularly interested in learning all I could about the life of Jesus Christ. If we were supposed to be Christians (Christ like), I wanted to know what that included. I began to talk to others about God and invite them to the Thursday night meetings at Bill's house. There was still a fire burning within me but this one was under control.

One Sunday at church, Bill came to me and said he had a girl the judge was willing to release into a home and asked if I would take her. The request caught me temporarily off guard.

"How long do I have to decide?" I asked.

"She gets out in two weeks," he replied. I told him I would think about it and let him know. At that point I didn't know to pray about every decision and wait for God to answer. Now that it was down to the nitty-gritty, did I really want to take in a girl from jail? All I knew was she had gotten in trouble and ended up in jail, then through the jail ministry program, had turned her life over to Christ and was now being allowed to move into a home. Our house was small and she would have to share a bedroom with the girls. How would they feel about that? When I shared the idea with the kids they were excited, even eager, to have a stranger share our home. I asked a couple of friends at church and they were apprehensive of such a move. Word got around to one of the elders wives. She called and scolded me for considering the idea, saying the girl would teach my children bad habits, probably steal us blind and most likely get my kids on drugs. When I reminded her that the girl had become a Christian, she made light of it, saying we didn't know her background. The only people who supported the idea were the group that met at Bill's house.

It was a heavy decision to make and it kept me awake several nights pondering it. On the one hand, I had always been concerned about not doing anything that upset the people around me, maybe too much so. On the other hand, I felt it might be the opportunity the young girl needed to get her life going in the right direction. One night as I lay awake, turning the problem over in my mind, I asked myself, what would Jesus do? Instantly I knew the answer. He would give the girl a home if he had one because he always met the needs of the people who asked. He left footprints and I would follow in them. I called Bill and told him I would take the girl.

The decision brought me an instant peace. Somehow, I felt liberated. I knew that I would never again allow what people thought, to stop me from doing what I was convinced God wanted me to do. Fear of people's opinions can be a paralyzing weapon and it no longer had a hold on me. Bill went with me to pick up the girl from jail. Her name was Linda and she was petite with long, fiery, red hair. She carried one paper bag of belongings and seemed nervous when we met. The guards told her to behave herself as we left the jail and walked across the parking lot to Bill's car. When we arrived at my house, she and the kids seem to hit it off right away. Bill talked to both of us about the rules. Linda would be allowed to do only what I agreed to. For one month, she could not go out unescorted. If she refused to follow the rules or ran away I was to simply notify Bill. The authorities would pick her up and she would go back to jail. Linda said she understood.

During the first few weeks, we all adjusted to living together and things went pretty smooth. Linda liked to read stories to the kids or play games with them and they all thought she was neat. Linda smoked, which I allowed her to do in the bathroom or outside. Much to my surprise, Linda said she had a ten-month-old, baby girl who lived with her mother. When she asked if Casey could come visit on weekends, I said sure and we all enjoyed the baby's visits.

Linda's dad had left home after she was born and never returned. Her mom had remarried several times but being a heavy drinker, she always married the same so Linda was raised in an environment of alcohol and its' victims. Linda felt the reason she got into trouble was because her mom never set any limits or taught her moral principles. When Linda became a teenager and somebody suggested doing something against the law, she went along with the crowd.

Linda studied the Bible with us and went with our family to church. She told the children how bad it was to be in jail and warned them about drugs. It seemed that Linda was a good influence, rather than a bad one, on the children. And she helped me learn not to be judgmental. How could I expect others to behave or react as I would consider proper or perhaps like I would behave or react, when their background or upbringing was so radically different to mine? After two months with us, one night, Linda went out and looked up her former boyfriend. He had a prison record and Linda was not allowed to see him. Someone reported it and Bill moved her to his house hoping she would follow the rules. After several weeks, Linda broke probation and ran away. Bill became depressed. It seemed his plan had failed and all our efforts had been wasted.

Life went on however and the church rented a house for boys from the streets. Two guys from the church moved in as overseers. Our Thursday night group helped out all we could. We cooked hot dinners at the house, conducted Bible studies and had beach parties with the boys. When I had taken in Linda against the advice of the elder's wife it had some negative results. Several ladies from the church who had visited us regularly, stopped coming to our home. Nothing was ever said about it and most were still friendly at church but they never socialized with us after that. It didn't bother me a lot. I knew I had done what Jesus would have done and would make the same choice again if the situation arose.

One cold, November night, the kids and I were helping make a spaghetti dinner at the boy's house. I saw a young, black boy there that I had seen around a few times before. When he wandered into the kitchen I introduced myself.

"Hi, I'm Jen," I said as I dried my hand on a towel and shook his.

"Cliff," he said," nice to meet you."

"Do you live here now?" I inquired.

"No, they are full up. No beds right now. I just like to hang around when I'm not working."

"Do you live nearby?" I questioned.

"Not exactly," Cliff replied," actually, I'm sort of living in my station wagon since my dad threw me out of the house."

"But don't you get cold at night?"

"Yeah, sometimes, I have a sleeping bag but sometimes I get cold."

He seemed like such a nice, young kid and I found myself wishing I could help him. I decided to find out more about his situation.

"How old are you and why did your dad throw you out?"

"I'm sixteen," he said. Hanging his head as if looking at a spot on the floor, a sad expression sobered his normally cheerful face, as he continued." And my dad was drunk and beatin' on Mom. I punched him to make him stop. He told me to leave and not come back, so I did."

"What about school?"

"I quit and got a job laying carpet. I make enough to eat and pay for my station wagon. I use it on my job. But I don't make enough to cover rent. Bill said when they have a place here, I can move in."

Later that evening, when Bill dropped by, I talked to him about Cliff. He said he was a good kid but they were jam packed and there was just no place to put him. I found Cliff and asked him if he would like to come stay at our house. We didn't have an extra room, I explained, but he was welcome to sleep in his sleeping bag on the living room floor or sofa. He would at least be warm and have a place to shower, shave and eat. He smiled and looked rather stunned.

"Do you really mean it?" He asked.

"Sure, why not?"

Cliff was the first black person that we had ever had in our home but after the first few days, I never thought of him as black. He was just Cliff. Just as Linda had made friends right away with the kids, so did Cliff. He loved to take them to the park or to McDonalds. They played touch football, basketball and board games. Cliff had several younger brothers and sisters and said he missed them. It was obvious that he loved kids. I encouraged Cliff to take a night program of studies that the school offered to complete high school and get his diploma. He took my advice. Cliff wasn't a Christian but he read the Bible and went to church with us. When he sat beside us and listed my address on the visitor's card, tongues began to wag. This time, lots of people began to avoid us. In their opinion we had really gone too far. We had taken in a black boy! Again, I knew I had done the right thing. Nothing makes you feel better inside than knowing you have done the right thing. I was tagged a radical but so was Jesus so I must be doing something right, I figured.

The Thursday night group was growing in leaps and bounds. It numbered around sixty. Young people were being saved off the streets and in the jails. Two jailers accepted Christ after seeing the changes in the prisoners. When a new sheep would join the flock, the telephones would begin to ring and we would gather at the church to sing and pray and baptize the new convert in the church baptistery. Sometimes these calls would come after midnight and we would stay and pray and sing until dawn. Usually, we had to work the following day. If someone got saved in jail, a policeman would bring them to the church for the baptism and afterwards take them back to jail.

One evening, when Cliff and the kids and I were reading the Bible at home, Cliff began to cry softly, saying," Jen, I want to pray and ask Jesus to come into my heart." Needless to say, it was a happy time at our house. We prayed with Cliff as he gave his life to Christ and called the gang to meet at the church for his baptism. The new Cliff began to pray for his father and soon he was able to go and talk things out with him. The family was happy to see him and asked him to move back home, which he did.

I began to hear talk here and there about "baptism of the Holy Spirit" and "unknown tongues". Our church taught that" unknown tongues" were of the devil and you received all of the Holy Spirit when you received Christ, that there was no such thing as a separate Holy Spirit baptism. But I saw Jesus in the lives of the people who said otherwise. They were obviously excited about living for Jesus and couldn't stop talking about him and the Bible. They shared their time and possessions with others. When I decided to investigate and ask questions, they gave me answers from the Scriptures. They more I investigated, the more I discovered the Scripture confirmed them both over and over in the early church.

At the time, we didn't have a washer and dryer at home so one Saturday afternoon, I made a trip to the local Laundromat. The place was deserted except for one very, unhappy looking, young man. He made some feeble attempts to begin conversation so after I started my laundry I sat down and talked with him. His name was Paul Miller and he seemed as unhappy as his face looked. After listening for a while to some of his problems with his job and his life, I decided to invite him to the Thursday meeting. I thought he might find answers as I had. I gave him my phone number and said if he decided to go to give me a call. He called later in the week with some excuse for not going. When he called again, he asked if he could come over and talk. I agreed and this was the beginning of our friendship. He liked to eat at our house, which he often did and enthralled the children with stories about the sea. He had been raised Catholic but admitted he had rejected that teaching and was in fact, agnostic. I kept talking up the Thursday meeting, feeling he would find love from the group and help for his problems and depression. After several weeks, he finally agreed to go but afterwards he said it wasn't for him and would never go again. I stopped inviting him but I didn't stop praying for him. At one point, when Paul was visiting and I was talking about something God had done, Paul huffily replied we could no longer be friends if I didn't stop all this religious stuff. I said if he felt that way we would just have to end our friendship. It wasn't long before he changed his mind.

Many months had passed since Linda had run away to California. One Sunday afternoon, the phone rang and it was Linda. She asked if she could come over and talk. When she arrived, she looked good. She looked happy. After we settled at the kitchen table with iced tea, she began to talk. She said after she got to California, she got back on drugs and into prostitution. She was picked up on a prostitution charge and sitting in the jail cell, when she thought of me. She said she tried to figure out why I had taken her from jail and into my home. She knew I didn't get money for it and I already had four kids to support, pick up after and care for. Why had I done it? She couldn't find an answer and then she remembered I told her it was the love of Jesus inside me that wanted to love and help her. She said she realized it had to be that and began to cry. She asked God to help her get her life straight again and give her the love of Jesus in her own heart. After she got out of jail, she went through a Christian rehab program and got off drugs. She met a nice man there and they were married and now both had come to Pensacola for her little girl, Casey.

"I want to thank you for loving me enough to take me in," she said." I know it was Jesus but you didn't have to do it and you did. If you hadn't, I probably would never have gotten my life together." Seeing Linda go straight and be happy was thanks enough.

5

Thank God for Laundromats

I was able to save $1000 our first year in Pensacola. A realtor found us a four bedroom townhouse, only two years old, that I could buy for a thousand down and assume a loan. Our payment would be $250 a month which I felt we could afford. When I took the kids to see it, the vote was unanimous. We wanted the townhouse. When our lease expired on our little cottage near the bay, we moved into our beautiful, new home. I opened a charge account with a large furniture store and bought new furniture for the living room and my bedroom. Heidi got my antique bedroom suite, Kim, a daybed because she wanted more space and my mother and dad sent money for bunkbeds for the boys. We spent hours choosing curtains and drapes, deciding on pictures and posters for the walls. Kim was eleven and beside herself, at the prospect of having a room of her own. The kids helped choose patterns and colors for their rooms so the decorating project was a happy, family event.

After a year in Pensacola, our lives drastically improved. Although we were far from being well-off financially and we never received the designated child-support payments, finances were no longer a problem. The calls and threats from Joe were rare. I had found a new internal peace although I was still searching for a deeper, closer relationship with God. The children were well and happy. One little thing still bothered me. I didn't have a husband and the children didn't have a father. I felt our little family was incomplete but I wasn't ready to trust another man. My heart and emotions were still far too bruised to risk further battering so I resigned myself to thinking romance could wait, maybe for a long, long time. When I would meet a man at work or church who seemed nice, I found myself thinking about what he was really like. Joe had been nice to me when we were dating. I knew all men were not potential wife beaters but I wasn't willing to find out which ones were not. When men asked me out, I just said I was recently divorced and not ready to date.

Bill spent a lot of time and effort with the growing group that met at his home. He seemed to get enjoyment from seeing all the changed lives. His wife, Lana, went along with all his efforts but less enthusiastically. When I could see the stress, I offered my home for the Thursday meetings to relieve some of the tension. It worked out fine. We continued to grow in numbers as God continued to move.

Our friend, Paul Miller, continued to visit but steered clear of the group meetings. In May, he called and asked if he could come over and talk. I knew from the sound of his voice that something was wrong. I wasn't prepared however, for the news that he had in store.

"Jen," he began," I have a problem."

"That's pretty obvious," I replied." What's wrong?"

"You know I worked at City Hall as programmer on the graveyard shift."

"Yes, what happened?" I asked.

"I got fired last week for oversleeping and going in late. It was the third time it had happened and they gave me the boot. I slept right through the alarm."

"That's terrible. What are you going to do, Paul?"

"Well, I've been looking for another job but that takes time and my roommate is kicking me out of the apartment because I won't have my half of the rent on the first. I was thinking, maybe I could move in with you and the kids just until I get on my feet again." Then he smiled and added," I know you take in strays occasionally."

My first thought was what people would say. Paul was not a kid. He was twenty-four years old. I knew there would be gossip. I told Paul I would think it over, pray about it and let him know in a few days. When I talked to the kids about it, Kim said she would give up her room and move in with Heidi, temporarily. That was a real sacrifice for her. She loved her private, little corner of the world. At Thursday's meeting, we prayed for guidance and without exception, all the group agreed it was God's will for me and the kids to take in Paul. That was my answer. Paul moved in and we welcomed him as a member of the family. He stayed with the kids on my school nights but went out with friends to play war games on Thursdays. He liked to cook and proved to be a lot of help around the house. On Sundays, he stayed home alone.

As always, God knows best and Paul's move to our house was no exception. Bill planned a weekend retreat for the youth in June. Several speakers and musical groups were coming from around the state and a large attendance was expected. I wanted to go but the retreat was for ages fifteen and over so I couldn't take the kids. I decided to invite Paul Miller to the retreat and thinking he would refuse, then, I would ask him to watch the kids for the weekend so I could go. A little reverse psychology was what I had in mind, thinking he would gladly babysit to avoid anything religious. Well, it was reverse all right, but on me. Paul, much to my surprise, said he would like to go to the retreat! I couldn't miss this, so I hired a sitter to stay with the kids and Paul and I went to the retreat together on Friday afternoon. Paul looked uncomfortable that evening but for me it was a fantastic time of worship and listening to testimonies of changed lives. One speaker was a professional, baseball player. Several young people offered their lives to Christ that Friday night. On Saturday, we broke up into small groups and I didn't see Paul except briefly at lunch. He was unusually quiet. Saturday afternoon as I headed for my dorm room to shower and change, Paul saw me from across the campus and called out to me. As he approached, I saw tears on his face.

"Paul, what's wrong?" I asked anxiously.

"I've decided to give my life to Jesus," he said," and I wanted you to know."

We hugged each other and wept together. When the crying was over, I wiped my eyes and looked at Paul. The pain and depression were gone from his face, replaced by a beautiful expression of peace that I had not seen before. So, it had really happened. God had chipped away the stone wall Paul had built around his heart.

"Jen, I've accepted Christ and I know my life will change but I'm never going to go around telling people about Jesus like you do. I'll live it but I won't broadcast it."

"It's okay, Paul," I replied." Whatever you want to do. I'm so happy for you. Your face has changed already."

"Yeah, I feel different. I feel good. Thanks for not giving up on me."

"I knew you were worth the effort," I said smiling.

On Sunday afternoon, Paul and several others were baptized in the lake at the camp and that evening, we went home, two, happy people. A few days later, while Kim and I were preparing dinner, the doorbell rang. Paul Miller answered it and announced it was an encyclopedia salesman. I said I wasn't interested. I already had a set. Paul responded he would like to see what the guy was selling and invited him inside. They talked at the dining room table. I stayed in the kitchen but couldn't help overhearing their conversation. The salesman was an Iranian selling encyclopedias to help pay his way through college. In a few moments, the conversation turned to religion. The young man said he was Islamic and explained briefly, what his beliefs were. Paul then asked him if he had heard of Jesus Christ.

"Yes," he replied." I have heard of him but know very little. What can you tell me about him?"

"Well, his story is written in what we call the Bible. Here," said Paul reaching for his Bible." Let me show you what it says."

When the young man left sometime later, Paul had not bought any encyclopedias but the salesman was carrying with him a paperback copy of the New Testament.

"Hey, Paul," I teased," I thought you weren't going to tell anybody about Jesus!" We both laughed.

"It's hard to keep it to your self," he said." Thank God for laundromats."

After the retreat, Paul soon found a job and moved into an apartment. He attended the Thursday night meetings regularly. At one of the meetings, he met Vicki, an elementary school teacher. They fell in love and were married later in the summer.

One day that summer, Bill called and invited me and the kids for Sunday dinner after church the following Sunday. Not having any plans, I accepted the invitation. When we arrived, I was introduced to an old school friend of Bill's, Sonny Maisfield. Sonny was an American airlines pilot and single. Over dinner, they swapped old stories about their youthful escapades and kept us laughing. It was a happy, noisy meal. After dinner, I began to clear the table and Bill, Lana and all the kids mysteriously disappeared into the backyard as if pre-arranged. Sonny helped me put away the food and load the dishes into the dishwasher. I was nervous, being alone with a single man. It brought up old, long forgotten feelings that were unsettling. But Sonny's warm, easy going manner and sense of humor soon helped me to relax. After we finished the cleaning up, Sonny said he promised his dad he would wash and polish the car he had loaned him. He asked if I would like to help. I had on a Sunday dress but thought, what the heck and agreed to help with the chore. After taking off my heels and hose I met him out front and we spent the afternoon washing and polishing and talking and laughing. I learned that Sonny was an adopted, only child and he had a deep respect for the parents who had given him a warm and happy home. He didn't come right out and say it but it was in the way he spoke of them.

After that Sunday, I never saw Sonny again. He flew back to California where he lived. But something changed inside of me that day. Somehow, the one afternoon with Sonny had melted away some of the fear I had inside and I realized I missed the companionship. I knew I was willing to try to find a lasting relationship, possibly a husband and father, try to find love. That Sunday night, thinking about Sonny, I wrote a short poem.

> His name is Sonny, he's quite a guy,
> Sometimes funny, sometimes shy.
> I'm glad we met and shared a day,
> Now he's gone, he flew away.
> A prayer I pray, though memories dim,
> Is may God always fly with him.

6

And God Can Save Professors

Little did I realize, that Sonny had unknowingly opened Pandora's box. I became somewhat obsessed with finding Mr. Right but my list of qualifications that he must possess was quite lengthy. I only dated men who I thought might qualify. I wouldn't date men who smoked anything other than a pipe or who drank liquor, regularly. I was looking for a Christian who was sensitive, caring and loved children. Obviously, this was a hard list to fill and usually you couldn't know a person until you dated a few months. But I began my campaign undaunted by these few obstacles.

Jim Brassell was the first prospect. He was a PhD Prof. of political science from the University of West Florida, located just on the northern outskirts of Pensacola. He came to our Thursday night meeting with Debbie, a student from one of his classes. Debbie was a regular in our group. Jim was tall, quiet, a bit shy, with reddish brown hair and wore glasses. His hair was longer than average, typical of the anti-establishment of the 70s. He had recently come through a painful divorce and professed a belief in God but did not believe Jesus was his son. Nobody pushed the issue and he continued to show up at the Thursday meetings. One night, Jim began to argue loudly and belligerently against the discussion of Scripture. It wasn't like him at all. When someone suggested we stop and pray, we all held hands and bowed our heads. Soon, Jim began to weep softly. The weeping turned into heavy sobs that shook his body. When it ended, he shared that he had had a revelation of Jesus as the son of God who died on the cross for mankind. Once again, I saw that look of peace on Jim's face that I had seen on Paul Miller's.

Several weeks later, after one of the meetings, Jim asked if I would like to go for a milkshake. I took him up on the offer. Debbie had gone for the summer to look up an old boyfriend. Jim was not handsome but the more I got to know him, the more I came to admire his sensitivity. We studied the Bible together and spent time together with the kids. I learned that Jim had always felt rejected by his father who was a wrestler and wanted a sports minded son. Jim was not athletic however, and his thing in life was reading and learning, resulting in a PhD. He had never been able to touch base with his father and it had become a thorn in the flesh, leaving him with a constant feeling of failure. We continued to see each other and although we were both afraid, we fell in love and talked seriously of marriage. Jim wanted to marry right away but I wanted to wait a few months to make sure we were doing the right thing. It proved to be a right decision. Jim's feeling of failure began to make him doubt his ability to be a good father to my children. We agreed to forget about marriage and eventually Jim married Debbie.

The next man in my life was Cary Milton, another professor from the same college. I met him at a party at a friend's house. My friend, Donna, was a secretary at the college. Cary was single so she invited him to her party. I disliked him, almost immediately. He came over and introduced himself and began a conversation. He was tall and handsome but obviously stuck on himself and very boastful about his accomplishments. Eventually, in the conversation, he asked me my philosophy of life.

"My philosophy? I guess it is loving God and allowing him to teach me to love others," I replied.

"Oh, you're one of those Jesus freaks," he said smugly.

"If that's what you want to call it," I said." I believe in God, Jesus, the Bible and the whole nine yards. Now, if you will excuse me, I really have to go." Agnostic egotism was not on my list of qualifications and I was glad to get away from Mr. Milton. I said good night to the hostess and went home. When I got inside, the phone was ringing. Kim answered it saying," Mom, it's for you." It was Cary Milton!

"How did you get my number?" I asked, not hiding the irritation in my voice.

"From Donna, are you upset?"

"Yes, I'm upset. What could you possibly want from a Jesus freak?" I responded.

"Oh, so I offended you with my terminology?"

"Just tell me why you called," I said.

"Well, I thought we might get together and talk some more about your philosophy."

"You've got to be joking," I replied.

"No, I'm serious."

"Well, the answer is no. I don't think you're interested in discussing Jesus. Now, good night Mr. Milton." I hung up the phone.

"Who was that, Mom?" Kim asked.

"Oh, just a joker I met at the party." I replied.

"Well, he must've said the wrong thing because you sure sound upset."

I hugged her and told her it was really nothing. After checking on the other children and tending to the sitter, I went upstairs to bed. It was a week later, when he called again. He apologized and made another attempt to see me. I again refused. On the fourth call, he said if I was really a Christian, I would forget our bad start and allow him to at least come over on Saturday and meet the children. Thinking that turning the children loose on him might be a good way to get rid of him, I finally agreed. It was a good plan but it didn't work. Cary liked the kids and they liked him. My kids liked most of the people they met. There were very few exceptions. They were well behaved, resulting in the people who met them nearly always, genuinely liked them and praised their behavior.

Cary had been married for six years when he was in his early twenties but had no children. I soon discovered that the "how great I am" exterior, was a mere cover-up for a lot of interior insecurities. Cary continued to visit regularly. I knew I would never marry a man who is not a Christian although I was becoming fond of him and he loved to do things with the kids. We all got used to having him around. I began to pray for God to save his soul but I didn't see any evidence of change in his beliefs. Cary was agnostic and pleased about it, or so he said. So our relationship had no visible future. After six months, Cary met a young girl at his apartment complex. They became interested in each other. We said our goodbyes and parted company. After Cary was gone from my life, I couldn't get him off my mind and continued to pray daily for God to somehow save his soul although I really felt, there was no hope.

All these months, I had continued to devour the Bible for answers. I couldn't seem to learn enough, fast enough. One Friday night, I had an unquenchable urge to go to church somewhere. But where? Our church had nothing going on Friday. On a whim, I checked the newspaper. A well-known Canadian evangelist, Brian Roudd, was holding revival at a large Assembly of God church in town. I had heard strange tales about" holy rollers" from such churches but decided to risk it and go. I got lost trying to find the church and arrived late. It was a large church, probably would seat a thousand and was almost full. I felt very uneasy in a strange church and decided to sit on a backseat near the door in case I wanted to leave in a hurry.

When the singing ended and Brian Roudd came out wearing a white, ruffled shirt and black, shiny pants, I would have bolted out the door but my feet seemed glued to the floor. Having been raised in a super conservative church, I had never seen a preacher in anything other than a suit and tie. As I listened to what he was saying, it sounded right on. He talked about how the devil deceives us with alcohol, drugs, riches, tobacco, lust, etc., and how our sin separates us from God and the devil moves in for the kill. He told of his own life of sin and how the devil tried to destroy him. He had been stabbed, involved with the Mafia, overdosed on drugs and all sorts of bad things until at one point, he made a failed attempt to kill himself in an isolation cell of a prison. It was there, he found Jesus or vice versa. His father was a preacher and despite a good Christian background, he had lived for the devil, much of his young life.

The church was packed with young people. When an altar call was given, over two hundred went forward for prayer. They began to toss cigarettes, drugs, porno books and all sorts of garbage upon the altar. It was an awesome sight to see two hundred young people fall on their knees and cry out for forgiveness before the Lord. They were taken by groups, into classrooms and counseled by church members or elders. After they had all left the altar, Brian Roudd began to point out different people in the audience and call them up front. To one man he said," God told me your wife left you and you've been praying for her return."

"That's correct," said the man.

"Well, God said, get ready, she's coming home real soon."

How did he know that man's wife left him I wondered? Nothing like this had ever happened in my church. It was exciting and mind-boggling. After he had called out several people and gave them all messages which he said were from God, he looked in the direction where I was sitting and pointing his finger, said," that lady on the backseat, come on down." I looked around to see who he meant. Everyone was looking at me. He couldn't mean me! I was just a curious spectator." Two seats from the aisle, in the wine colored jacket." I looked up and there was that finger pointing directly at me. The people around me began to urge me to go on down. It was too late to escape. By now, everyone was looking at me and waiting for me to go forward. Petrified, I stood up slowly and walked to the front.

"Young lady," he began," God has a message for you." I tried not to collapse and make a spectacle of myself.

"You have been praying for a young man. You're concerned about his soul. Is that right?" Immediately, I thought of Cary.

"Yes, that's right," I replied

"Now listen closely," he continued." God wants to use you to prophesy and this is how you will know that this message is from God and not from me. You go home and call that young man and tell him he is about to be saved and filled with the Holy Ghost. Will you do it?" He asked. I said I would. I would've agreed to sit on top of a flagpole to get off of that podium just then. Somehow, my legs carried me back to my seat and soon the service ended.

Driving home, I began to think about what Brian Roudd had said to me. I didn't really know what prophesy meant. I would have to check it out. And I could just see me telling Cary he was going to be saved and filled with the Holy Ghost. For that matter, I really didn't even know what it meant to be filled with the Holy Ghost. I knew it was more than just being saved and when you had this baptism you could speak in other languages. Surely, I thought, Brian Roudd must have been mistaken but then how did he know I was praying daily for Cary's soul. The next few days I couldn't get that message off my mind. I would wake at night thinking about it but I could not find the courage to call Cary and give him such a message. So I continued to agonize over the situation. Nine days after the strange, Friday night at the Assembly of God, my birthday came along. It was on Sunday. After church, when I was ready to load the kids in the car and go home, I couldn't locate David. The other children helped me search and eventually we found him hiding beneath a pew. He had no explanation for his strange behavior and we went on home. When I opened the door, thirty-five friends came out of hiding, shouting" happy birthday". It was definitely a surprise. I was thirty-two and although I had enjoyed lots of birthday cakes I had never had a party. I was so surprised and happy that I cried. Kim, with the help of the other kids had planned it all. She had made me a cake and punch and all the guests brought a covered dish. They even thought of hiding David so everyone could beat me home and surprise me. Then I saw him standing beside the kitchen door, smiling. Kim had invited Cary and there he stood. I thought of the message but could I bring myself to tell him? A voice began to shout inside my head," you have to tell him."

"Okay, okay," I answered silently. If he stays around until the others leave, I will tell him." I hoped he would leave early but he didn't. This business of doing what God wants is tough sometimes, I thought. After lots of eating and talking and laughing, slowly the guests began to leave. When they had all gone except Cary, and only God could have so conveniently arranged that, we were alone in the dining room.

"Cary," I began haltingly." I'm going to tell you something strange that happened. I know you're going to laugh but save it all until I'm finished, okay?" Looking puzzled but curious, he agreed. Then I told him the whole story, the urge to go to church somewhere, anywhere, the strange preacher and last of all the words the preacher spoke to me.

"Now that's it, you can laugh about it." He didn't laugh.

"Well," he said as if trying to muster up something humorous but couldn't," when is all this supposed to happen to me?" I couldn't tell if he was poking fun or serious.

"Soon," I replied." He said it would happen real soon."

"Well, Jen," he said, pushing his chair away from the table and standing," I enjoyed your party but I have to go now and if I get saved, I assure you, you will be the first to know." With that he kissed me gently on the cheek and said goodbye. I still didn't know how he had received the message but it didn't matter anymore. It had been a long but happy day and I was tired. I had finally relayed that agonizing message and tonight I could get some sleep. After Cary was gone and I was clearing away some of the leftover party, I realized how much I missed having him around. One thing was sure, this finding Mr. Right was not going to be easy!

Two weeks after my birthday, the phone rang in the middle of the night. At first I didn't recognize the voice because of the sobbing. When it finally registered, it was Cary.

"Jen," he said," tonight, I met your Jesus." I waited as he broke in with more sobbing, "and I got the baptism and the tongues and the whole package. I promised you would be the first to know. I know it's late and I'm sorry to wake you but I just couldn't wait to tell you. Please forgive me for all the bad times I gave you about your faith." After he hung up, it was difficult to believe it really happened. God had saved Cary Miller and filled him with the Holy Spirit just like Brian Roudd had said he would. It was too good to be true. It meant that God still actually talks to his sheep who have tuned their ear to hear and if God could save Cary Miller he could save most anybody. What a lot that was for my mortal mind to absorb. Wow! My search for answers was paying off in a way I never dreamed. I went to sleep, smiling and thinking that tomorrow I would have to learn what it meant to prophesy.

7

Published Praise the Lord

When spring came around that year of '72, I took golf and tennis lessons at the college. I bought tennis rackets for all the kids and taught them to play. We spent a lot of hours that summer on the tennis courts. Even David, who was only four, liked the game all except the part of chasing balls that got away. I loved to golf and coaxed my girlfriend, Pat, into learning the strokes so we could enjoy the game together. I didn't count on her becoming hog-wild about it. She couldn't seem to get enough of hitting that little, white ball around the course. One Saturday morning when the phone rang at seven-thirty and I was still sleeping, it was Pat. She said there was a big pro-am tournament, starting at eight, at the Pensacola golf course and wanted me to go with her to watch. Reluctantly, I crawled out of bed and into the shower. When I went downstairs, Paul had let her in and she was waiting for me in the kitchen. Paul liked to get up early and always had a pot of coffee made, knowing I couldn't function without my morning coffee. I thanked him, gave him a big hug and wrote the number of the golf course on a pad beside the phone. Kim was eleven and Paul nine. Occasionally I left them on their own for a few hours. Our friend, Eddie, from church, was coming at noon, to take them all to fly kites in the park. I grabbed a cup of coffee and Pat hauled me off to the golf course.

When we arrived, there were only a handful of spectators. The smart ones were still home in bed, I thought, where I would like to be. We were standing under a big oak watching the antics of two squirrels when a stray ball rolled off the fairway into the grass. When two men came over in a cart, looking for the elusive ball, we showed them where it landed. That's how we met Johnny Unitas. Later, when the round was finished and he saw us standing in the gallery, he took us to meet Lee Majors. It was a fun and exciting day. For months, David told virtually everybody, that his mom had met the six million dollar man.

I had met Pat at one of my evening college classes. She was young and attractive but always quiet and withdrawn. Thinking that maybe she could use a friend, I approached her one evening after class and introduced myself. She seemed a bit hesitant to talk to me so I gave her my phone number and told her to call me sometime and we would get together. She smiled and thanked me and we went home. Months later, I got a call from Pat and she asked if we could go for lunch. I met her at a restaurant the following day and she opened up a little. She told me she was recently divorced and had been depressed over it. She didn't have anyone to talk to. I knew where she was coming from, having experienced the same thing. I invited her over for the following Saturday and before long we were close friends. It was almost a year before she shared that the first night she called me, she had planned to end her life with a bottle of tranquilizers. She couldn't cope with the depression and she had no one to talk to. She put the pills on the nightstand and was writing a final note when she remembered I had given her my phone number. That's when she called. It gave me chills to think that such a simple act could save a life. It also increased my awareness and sensitivity to unhappy, depressed people. Pat introduced to me to community theater. I had taught her golf which she loved and I felt the same about the theater. The end result was a lot of happy times for both of us.

That year, I met Eric Walls, the producer-director of the local educational TV channel. We both liked to write and Eric enjoyed the community theater. It looked as if our relationship had a chance at being long-term. He even drove out to Texas with me in August to pick up the kids who had flown out and spent six weeks on my folk's farm. But after a few months it all began to fall apart. He believed in God and went to church on occasion but being a Christian was not a high priority on his list. Eric disliked the ocean, the beach and the sun which was a big part of mine and the kids' lives. So, reluctantly we gave it up as a lost cause but remained friends.

In one of my evening, English classes, after several writing assignments were returned, all with red penciled A's at the top, my professor approached me and asked if I was a professional writer.

"Goodness, no," I replied," Why would you ask that?"

"It's just that your writing is good, good enough to be professional," he said. I didn't know what to say. I had written several poems and made A's in English during high school but had no idea I had real writing talent.

"Have you considered trying to sell a story?" He asked.

"Why, no, I would have no idea how to begin."

"Well, you should consider it. Bring one of the stories you've written for my class to the office sometime and I will help you get started."

"Okay, I will," I said, flabbergasted." Thanks."

When I saw Eric later, I told him what the professor had said. He seemed pleased and offered to look over the stories and make some suggestions. After checking them out, we selected a true story that had happened in Mineral Wells. Joe's construction company had a contract with a brick factory to dig out the clay on top of Welcome Mountain with a front end loader, load it onto a large Mack truck and deliver it down the winding road to the clay pit below at the factory. One week, Joe was out of town and left me in charge to make sure everything kept moving at the contract site. On Monday morning, the dump truck driver didn't show. If we didn't meet our quota for the day, our contract would be canceled. I couldn't find the driver or a replacement so I asked Jude, the loader operator, to show me how to change the gears and release the dump on the Mack dump truck. He didn't think I could handle it. I weighed one hundred and twenty pounds, soaking wet but I drove the truck and managed to get the load down the hill and back the wheels onto that skinny ramp, over the pit. All morning, things went smooth without a hitch. I was scared and nervous but I knew I had to do it. Just before noon, Jude filled the truck and signaled it was ready. The truck was idling in neutral. When I pushed in the clutch, to put the truck in gear, it began to roll forward. I pumped the air brake to stop it until I could get it in low gear for the downhill descent but the brake pedal hit the floor. There was no brake. I fought an overwhelming urge to panic as I tried to force the gear into position to slow the truck but without any luck. With several tons of clay and a downhill winding road, the truck was soon moving so fast I couldn't hold onto the wheel. At the bottom of the hill, the road made a 90° turn to the right toward the factory. Right across the road, staring me in the face, was an old, steel railroad car. It didn't take much figuring to know if I didn't turn over before I reached the bottom of the hill, I would smash, smack dab into that railroad car. Either way, I would die. So when I lost control of the wheel, I said a hasty prayer asking God to watch over my children. I didn't think even he could get me out of this one. I laid my head forward on the wheel so I didn't have to watch myself die and waited.

At the foot of the hill, was a large mud hole, rare for that time of year in north-central Texas. The truck did a series of crazy spins when it hit the mud hole full speed and ended up behind the railroad car, never touching it. I climbed out of the truck and into another one and finished out the day, thus ending my brief, truck driving career. When the truck was eventually examined, it was discovered that the air hose had somehow gotten disconnected, causing the brakes to fail. People came out of the factory all afternoon, shaking their heads in disbelief, when the story got around. Everyone who saw where the runaway truck came to rest called it a miracle and indeed it was.

When Eric read the story, he suggested I send it to GUIDEPOSTS. The monthly magazine publishes true life dramas with a spiritual message. After retyping the story, I took it to the professor. He agreed GUIDEPOSTS was a good choice and helped me write a cover letter to the editor. I put it in the mail that afternoon. Most of my friends advised that it was very difficult to get your first story published and cautioned me not to get overly excited about the prospect. When nothing happened after several weeks, I thought my friends must be right and forgot about it. Some two months later, I received a call from the magazine editor. It was the beginning but after several phone conversations, they agreed to buy and publish my story. When it was edited, they made a lot of changes that made me look stronger and braver than I felt at the time. I agreed to the changes, however and the magazine made arrangements for a photographer to come to Pensacola and shoot pictures for of the story.

On Friday night, the photographer, Martin Rowes, called, saying he was in Miami and would be in Pensacola at ten the following morning. I agreed to meet him at the airport. He requested that I try to locate a Mack dump truck for the pictures. On Saturday morning I had only one stop to make before going to the airport. I allowed ample time to drop off Heidi's flute for new pads at the music store. When I got back into the car, a new one by the way, it wouldn't start. It took twenty minutes to find a volunteer with battery cables to get me on the road again. I knew if I missed the plane it could spoil the whole day. By the time I arrived, the plane had already landed and some of the passengers disembarked. As I desperately scanned the passengers around the luggage pickup station, I saw one man with a Kodak hanging around his neck but he had to be a tourist.

The only other man carrying a large camera case strapped over his shoulder was carrying a parka. You wouldn't need a parka in Miami, I deducted. Disappointed, I sat down on a bench to think. Soon a voice from behind me asked," Would you be Jennifer Jireh?" I stood to face the man with the parka.

"Yes, but how did you know?" I asked, puzzled." I didn't give you a description on the phone, and the parka, why a parka in Miami?"

He smiled and replied," when no one was waiting to meet me at the plane, I just called your house. Your kids told me what you looked like and what you were wearing. And the parka, well, before I arrived in Miami this week, I was working on pictures for a story in Russia."

That explained everything. I told him about the problem with the car as we made our way to the parking lot. Knowing that this man traveled around the world to do photography, made me edgier than before but Martin Rowes proved to be one of the most laid back, easy going, people I had ever met. He was tall and handsome, about forty and recently married to an airline hostess. I asked what time his flight departed and he said four.

After meeting the kids and shooting several rolls of film of us around the house, I offered to make lunch but he insisted on taking us out to eat. The kids voted for Red Lobster so we loaded into the car. David wanted to sit on Martin's lap which was perfectly agreeable to him. I could hardly watch the road, as David toyed with the camera and asked a million questions but it didn't seem to bother Martin at all. At the restaurant, he took more pictures while we were waiting for our order. People were watching and the kids were having fun but I was embarrassed by all the attention. I told Martin I had located a trucking company that was willing to let us use a truck for the pictures but it was ten miles from town. I suggested that we go there after lunch.

"What, and miss the beach?" he said." I bet you kids would like to go to the beach."

"Yeah, let's go to the beach," was the unanimous reply.

After wading in the surf, digging in the sand and climbing mango trees, atop the dunes, all of which he captured on camera, once again, I suggested we go do the truck shots. I didn't want him to miss his plane. He agreed, but took a lot more shots before we finally headed back to the car. At the trucking company, we met the manager who escorted us to a Mack dump truck, where we began the pictures. Soon, a crowd gathered to watch. It was getting late and we had a long drive to the airport but Martin kept saying," just a few more, try to look tense now. You're coming down that hill and the brakes have failed." I was tense so that part was not hard at all! At a quarter of four, he finally finished and I tried to hurry everybody to the car. We were miles from the airport. I sped through yellow lights, zig-zagged in and out of traffic and at one major intersection, the car in front of me stalled, while waiting for the light to change. I was in the inside lane, traffic on the right of me was too steady to break into. Any second, the light would change to red again. I jerked the car to the left, over the curb and around the disabled car. A few minutes later, we went screeching tires, into the airport loading zone. The plane was loading with a few final passengers boarding.

"Well, I guess we made it," I said breathlessly.

"I never doubted that we would," Martin said calmly." I knew that any lady who could drive a Mack dump truck could get me to the airport on time." He shook my hand, said goodbye to me and the kids and was the last to board the plane. On the stairwell he turned to wave.

8

And the Winner's Number Seven

For years, I had been plagued by sinus, allergy headaches but other than that my general health had been good. But in '72 that began to change. One day at work, I had a severe attack of chest pain and fainted. After days of tests in the hospital, the culprit was discovered to be diverticulitis. The doctor put me on a seedless, nutless diet and I soon improved. Next, came a series of bladder and kidney infections. Usually antibiotics would bring them under control but one evening while painting the hall walls, I suddenly became feverish and nauseous. The children were all outside playing. Feeling faint, I went upstairs to lie down. I soon became too sick to go outside and find the children so I dialed a friend to come over. When she arrived, I was delirious from the fever. At the hospital emergency, albumin was found in the blood stream. The doctor said I would have died in a matter of hours without large doses of antibiotics.

I began to remember my request for God to allow me five more years of life. It had been five years. I began to pray daily for an extension. The children still needed me and I had so much left to do. He must have agreed because I didn't die. I worked in a small, engineering office with one machinery designer, one project engineer and myself. We were pretty close and shared a lot of our personal lives with each other. One day, Marty, the engineer, invited me to visit his church. It was classified as inter-denominational but many of the members had received the baptism of the Holy Spirit. I decided to check it out. On Sunday, after the song and worship service, someone stood and gave a message in a language I did not understand. Another, gave an interpretation in English. The interpretation was a message from God to the congregation. I was amazed to think God would communicate this way to the people.

After the sermon, an invitation was given to come forward to receive the baptism of the Holy Spirit. I wanted it. I was convinced it would enable me to get closer to God. The Bible says that unknown tongues make it possible to communicate directly from the heart to God(Rom.8:26). I went up front with a few others. A group gathered around us and laid hands on us and asked God to give us the baptism. Some began to speak in strange languages, some began to weep but I had no apparent manifestation. The people around me assured me that I had received the baptism and tongues would come later. They told me to simply trust God. I was a bit disappointed, but convinced that it meant more of God and would wait as long as necessary for the new language. It was almost a month, before it happened. I was alone in my bedroom, praying, when strange noises came bubbling out of my mouth. I got so excited I couldn't stop and prayed and sang in this new language into the night until I became hoarse and literally lost my voice. I had never been more consumed with pure joy.

Kim, Paul and Heidi continued to do well in school. When Kim entered the eighth grade, she took a state wide aptitude test and finished in the upper 15% bracket. The test result made her eligible for one of several, extracurricular programs outside the school. She chose a photography course at the Pensacola Naval base. It was an excellent course in picture taking, black and white and color development, cameras and virtually everything related to photography. Paul and Heidi excelled in art. They both won numerous awards with their artwork. Paul was chosen for the tennis team and Heidi took baton and played flute in the band. David finished kindergarten without problems but encountered difficulties in the first grade. It wasn't discovered until the second grade that he had dyslexia. It affected him in two areas. He sometimes saw letters and pictures backwards and if instructed to do three things, could only remember one or two. He repeated the second grade and was put into a special program to help overcome the problem. He soon became an avid reader but hated homework and that area became a battleground.

During those months, after prayer for the baptism of the Holy Spirit, a number of changes took place. Some were drastic. Some were subtle. One night, while praying, God spoke to me and requested two things, all my fears and my children. He asked me to release them totally into his hands. I had a lot of fears, whole lists of them. My parents loved us but tended to over protect us, especially the younger ones. They were afraid of swimming, we might drown. If we climbed a tree we were sure to break a leg. Riding in cars with friends, meant accidents. Walking in the woods, spelled snakebite. Many of their fears came from losing Kenneth and Wanda but others had been passed down to them. Dad was sorely afraid of storms. Nearly every place we lived, we had a storm cellar. When the dark clouds threatened, we would head to the cellar, which was always equipped with cots and blankets, fresh water, lantern and axe. I can easily recall the musty, earthen odor mixed with that of the burning coal oil from the lantern. Canned fruits and vegetables from last summer's labor lined the shelves along the walls. If you looked closely you could always find, hidden in some discreet corner, a black widow spider, tending her egg. I was deathly afraid of spiders, especially black widows. The cellar was a favorite dwelling, too, for Texas rattlers. Dad would check it regularly to keep the viper population at a minimum and always, a check was in order before we entered.

When I was growing up, I remembered thinking that when I had children, I wasn't going to teach them to be so afraid of living. In some areas, I had succeeded. I had overcome any fear of snakes and spiders in the woods. I allowed the children to climb and didn't hover over them protectively as I noticed some of my sisters doing. But I had added a few to the list, and had enough fear inside me to cripple me for life. I was afraid to release all my fears to God, after all, I had known them since childhood. They were so much a part of me but I finally agreed to surrender them. But the children were a different matter. I was afraid to let them go. I wanted to think about that first. It was about a week of inner turmoil before I decided to surrender total control of my children to God. Almost instantly, I had a peace about the decision, once it was made.

Those two steps changed my life. I discovered a new direction of thought patterns. For instance, I no longer needed a savings account. I trusted God to provide daily, even if I lost my job. I used the money to help others as God showed me their needs. And insurance, became to me, a lack of trust in God. I only kept what the company provided for free or what was required by law. It seemed to me that God could only protect me in the areas that I trusted him to do so. When I purchased any un-required insurance policy, it was like saying to him that it was just in case he didn't come through if the need arose. I know your word says you will guide, keep, protect, provide, cover, heal, love, feed, clothe and lots more, but just in case you don't, I will lay aside a little nest egg or keep this little policy to tide me over. For me, it became all or nothing in trusting God. There was no middle ground. It didn't all happen at once and life didn't become instant paradise but it sure became easier to live, to cope and to make decisions. I simply consulted God in prayer and in the Bible. With me, God had a big job on his hands. I needed a complete overhaul. My mind was filled with a lot of misconceptions about him and about his word. I had a lot of pride and vanity. I was always thinking that I should get a Masters degree or PhD. But God began to show me, through his word, that it wasn't more knowledge that I needed but wisdom to use the knowledge I had, to help others. I began to change my style of dress. Sometimes, I had dressed to attract attention but I no longer needed that. Slowly and gently, God began to show me little things, wrong with my life. The decision was always mine. I could change or remain status quo. Usually, after careful thought and prayer, I chose to drop the ugly little things that God exposed.

The Bible speaks about being born again and seeing with new eyes and hearing with new ears. That's exactly what happened to me. It was as if I could see things more as God sees them, hear things more as God hears them and feel things more as God feels them. As I slowly changed inside, it resulted in changes on the outside. Changes don't happen overnight and they won't stop until we go home to the father. Some Christians change little or none at all. When God shines light on a certain area, some prefer to stay in darkness and never grow. Each time that God showed me an area that needed improvement, if I followed through, and with his help made the change, soon he would show me another area that needed work. The rough edges that needed sanding usually hurt a bit, sometimes a lot, but after it was over, I always looked back and wondered why I had held on to that thing so long and stubbornly.

He began to speak to me about my time. He suggested if I gave up some of the time I spent on myself, sailing or golfing, I would have more time to help others. At first, I resisted rather strenuously. I loved sailing and golfing and figured I deserved those treats. But soon, I began to wonder what God had in store for me if I gave them up. Eventually, I decided to find out. Always, it was something to help someone and I got a special feeling of satisfaction and fulfillment in doing it. Soon, I found I was doing very little golf, attending the theater on rare occasions and not at all upset about the changes in my life.

Meanwhile, David kept asking for a dad and despite my fruitless efforts, I kept hoping and trying. I explained to him that it wasn't like ordering something from a catalog. You didn't just choose the size and model you wanted and have it delivered in the mail. It took time and patience and a lot more. But David made no secret about the fact that he wanted a daddy like other kids had. I tried to make up for the lack of a father in his life as much as possible. He belonged to Cub Scouts and when I picked him up after his meeting one day, he had an entry blank for a father-son, kit, stock car race. The rules explained you purchased a kit which consisted of one, small block of pine and two sets of plastic wheels. From this, you designed, carved and assembled a racecar. The rules included a maximum weight limit and said you could paint or finish the car however you chose. The race would consist of racing the cars down narrow, plastic tracks. The car that crossed the finish line first at the bottom in each division would win. Then the division winners would compete for top prize. David was upset because he didn't have a daddy to help and couldn't enter the race. I told him, I would help build the car and we would enter the race. We bought our kit and turned in our entry form. A few days later, I got a call from the Scout leader saying he was sorry, but women were not allowed in the competition. It sort of rubbed me wrong.

"Listen, David doesn't have a dad and this is his competition, not mine. Now you can tell the leaders that David is entering that race if I have to take it to the national headquarters and I am going to help, because I'm all he has right now and if your dads feel threatened, well that's just too bad." I hung up, very upset. Living without a father, I felt, was punishment enough for innocent children. To be denied the normal right of having fun and entering competition, because of it, was unthinkable to me. A few days later, I got another call saying someone had decided we could enter.

We got our little, wooden block and with Paul's pocket knife, carved out a little hole where the seat should be. We rounded off the front and rear a bit and cut two slots across the bottom for the wheel shafts. Next, we stapled the shafts to the wood to keep them from falling off. After a few licks with sandpaper to smooth the rough edges, we then painted the number seven, on the hood. Seven was the number assigned to our car with the entry blank. Paul suggested we print," bye,bye sucker" and "move over for a winner" on the sides of our super hot Rod. We were all pleased with the results of our efforts, and using a piece of plastic racetrack, we made a downhill ramp and gave number seven a trial run. She went flying to the bottom and we were sure we had a winner.

On the evening of the competition, which was at a local elementary school, all of the family wanted to go, as well as the latest man in my life, Ray Jameson, an engineer. David was as excited as at Christmas time. It was all he had talked about for days. When we entered the gymnasium where the downhill tracks had been set up, my heart sank. The room was full of fathers and sons, looking proud and excited, which was understandable, but it was the cars that upset me. Without exception, every car I saw, was carved to perfection, into miniature replicas of Porsches, Ferraris and other different styles and models, all painted with real, metallic, car paints and lettered and numbered with stencils. I was suddenly ashamed of our pitiful, plain number seven. I had the car inside my purse so David wouldn't break the wheels before the race. He began to ask for the car to show it off, apparently unaware of the difference in the cars. The other kids and Ray looked at me. It was plain to see they were thinking what I was thinking. Heidi was first to put it into words.

"Mom, those other cars don't look like ours, do they?"

"No, honey, they don't." I replied. I couldn't put David off any longer. Slowly, I pulled out number seven and handed it to him. Soon, the snickers began around the room. Most everyone was looking at our plain, little car and many of them were laughing. They were getting even with me for insisting on entering the race.

"Mom, why are they laughing at our car?", David asked innocently.

"Because they don't know any better. It's okay. We will win and have the last laugh," I said, trying to make him feel better, but I couldn't convince myself number seven had a chance.

"Weigh in time," a man called out, standing near a small scale on a table. The boys lined up and weighed their cars. Our car was a couple of ounces under the maximum allowed weight. Ray suggested we tape some coins in the carved out seat to give it more speed. I found some masking tape in my purse and we added three pennies. Number seven looked even funnier. There were twenty-five entries and three different divisions. When it came David's turn, we all shouted encouragement. I was as shocked as all the scoffers, when number seven beat the competition to the bottom of the track. For a moment, no one but David could believe it.

"And the winner of this division is number seven, owned by David Jireh," the announcer said." Now, will all be winners get ready for the final race, for the first, second and third-place trophies." In the final heat, number seven took home the second place trophy for the entire race. David was livid with joy. On our way out, lots of little boys congratulated David. Even some of the fathers shook our hand and offered a word of congratulations. I didn't hear a single snicker!

9

Goodbye Daddy

At our church, the Thursday night group was causing quite a stir. Some of the hard-core conservatives, didn't want any longhairs, ex-druggies and former prostitutes in their midst. Never mind the fact that those were exactly the types that Jesus hung out with. And they conveniently, overlooked the minute detail that they had accepted Christ as Savior, their sins, forgiven, their pasts behind them. They still didn't want them in the church. One morning, I overheard an elder's wife say," What is all this riffraff doing in our church?" Funny, I thought. I was under the impression that it was Jesus's church and he always welcomed the riffraff with open arms. It was the self-righteous hypocrites he had a problem with.

Soon, there were complaints about our hugging and holding hands during prayer. We were informed it was lustful and would have to cease. Also, a large amount of money was donated to the church specifically designated for purchase of the boy's house that the church had been renting. The elders decided to use it for something else. Bill was angry and hurt and quit going to church. Before long, the Thursday group disbanded. Bill became discouraged when several went back to their old habits and without Bill as a leader, the group dissolved. Many continued on with Christ but went to other churches and prayer groups for fellowship. One thing was accomplished. Our church was rid of all its riffraff. I loved many of the people at my church and was so alive and excited about my new life since the baptism of the Holy Ghost, that I stayed at the church and tried to help others see what a treasure the kids and I had found. After about a year, I realized it was a futile effort and changed to the church that Marty attended, on the beach. It was much smaller and I was free to worship God uninhibited.

At work, after three years, things were going great. I had been made company artist which meant I got to plan and oversee product exhibits at county fairs and seminars. At Christmas time, Armstrong had a giant extravaganza for employees and their families. Each year, we picked a different theme and, using a company warehouse, we spent weeks planning, building, decorating and arranging for caterers to feed the thousand plus people who would attend. Decorations were my job and I loved it. Once, we built a gingerbread cookie booth for Santa, to take requests from children. Wooden reindeer, led a red sleigh-covered tractor that gave visitors rides around the plant. I had also been assigned reporting duty for the company bulletin we published weekly. I liked staying busy and on the move. Then one day, our boss, Bob Dell, plant engineer, told us that he would be out for two days. He was checking into the local hospital for tests. Bob was never one to share himself or his problems so nobody asked any questions. We simply wished him the best. The next day, Marty, George, and I were called to the plant manager's office. He sadly informed us that Bob was dead. We were all very shocked by the unexpected news. Bob was only forty-four and seemed to be in very good health. I never remember him missing a day's work and now, he was dead! He had an arteriogram, a tube inserted into the artery to discover any heart related blockages in the system. The test had revealed a blockage and surgery would be required to open up the artery. Only a few hours after the test, Bob had a fatal heart attack. It was assumed, the tube dislodged tissue which entered the bloodstream causing the fatal heart attack. Mr. Hufford, the plant manager, expressed his grief, at losing a wonderful employee and good friend. He said a search would begin immediately for someone to take Bob's place but in the meantime, Marty would become temporary plant engineer, George, who preferred the office to the field, would do designs and paperwork and I would cover Marty's projects in the plant and outside on the grounds. He said he knew it would be a difficult time for us but expressed his confidence in our abilities to handle the engineering department alone.

Bob's funeral was extremely sad. He was a happy, hard-working man. He was quiet and almost always, smiling. Hundreds turned out to pay last respects. He left behind a wife and three teenage children. His wife asked George and Marty to be pallbearers and asked me to walk behind the casket as honorary pall bearer. I felt it was thoughtful of her not to leave me out, although I was the only woman in the group.

The weeks turned into months and still no replacement was named to take Bob's place. The three of us stayed very busy and I enjoyed the new assignment.

It was a challenge. If I had questions, I went to Marty. If Marty had questions, he contacted a consultant engineer. One day, my project sheet listed the order for twenty truck loads of clay for a ground fill project. It gave the location where the clay was to be delivered and dumped. I called a local dirt contractor and ordered the twenty loads of clay. He said they would deliver the following day. I left word for the guard at the gate house to call me when the first delivery arrived. The next day, when the guard called, I went down to the gatehouse to show the driver where to unload. When I introduced myself and offered to get in the cab to show the way to the unloading site, the crotchety, old man said he didn't do business with women. I thought he was a real donkey but simply replied," Sir, with all due respect to your feelings, this is my job and I can show you the site and sign your delivery ticket the same as a man." In a patronizing effort, he smugly countered," Look, honey, I only do business with men. Now call me a man out here." I stepped inside the gatehouse and paged Marty. When he arrived a few minutes later, I explained the situation. Marty thought about it a moment, then stepped up to the truck and introduced himself to the driver.

"Are you the owner of this hauling company?" Marty asked.

"Sure am," the old man replied, grinning, to expose tobacco stained teeth.

"Then," continued Marty," I guess we'll have to find another company because this job will take several days and we don't have a man to work with you and you don't want to work with this lady and it's her job." I could always count on Marty to back me up against men who thought I should be home baking cookies. They couldn't know, I never wanted the working world and was trying to support my kids the best way I knew how.

"Well," the old man said ducking his head and clearing his throat." In that case, we'll just have to make do. Get in little lady and show me where to dump."

After three months, we were notified a new man had been selected from the Pennsylvania plant to take Bob's place. He was young, married and his name was Larry Bonner. From the beginning, we didn't hit it off. Like the truck driver, he thought I was out of my place doing all the different jobs around the plant that I had inherited. He stopped my artwork, canceled my reporting, gave most of my drafting design to George and set me down at a desk with his paperwork. He had to share a secretary with another department which he didn't like, so he made me his private secretary. I hated the work. I felt trapped and imprisoned. Bookkeeping, record keeping and typing have always been some of my least favorite things. A year earlier, when I had visited the main plant and headquarters in Pennsylvania, the head of the art department there offered me a full-time job. A few months after Bob's death, I called to see if the offer was still open. Learning that it was, I applied for a transfer to the Lancaster, Pennsylvania plant. Larry Bonner stopped it, saying my job title was not important enough for the company to transfer me to another plant. He convinced Hufford it would set a precedent and other peons would be requesting transfers. So a few months later, I put my house up for sale and resigned. I enrolled for the next semester at the local college to work toward an art degree. It wasn't what I wanted but I couldn't sit and do Larry Bonner's paperwork anymore. He had taken all the joy out of my job and I hated going to work in the mornings.

One of the elders of the little church I was attending was a former senator and owned a real estate-insurance company. When I asked him about listing my townhouse, he said he could get me a quick sale if I would deduct $1000 from the appraised value. I agreed and he drew up a contract. Real estate prices had greatly increased since I bought the place and my equity would amount to around $10,000. I calculated it would be enough to finish college and to live on for a while. In the meantime I could pick up some more odd jobs.

The weeks dragged into months and still no sale on the townhouse. No one ever came around to look at it. When I asked the elder, he said he just hadn't found the right buyer but assured me that he would. Then, I met a Christian singer, Jack Jackson, who said he would like to buy the house. His house in Colorado was under contract and when it closed he would be able to buy mine. He asked if he could move into my place and make the payments until the sale, to save him an extra move. It was the beginning of summer and my folks wanted the kids to come to the farm in Texas for a month or so as they usually did. Kim had braces put on that spring and the orthodontist didn't want her to go, as he had to make frequent checks and adjustments so she planned to stay with me in Pensacola. We made a quick trip to Texas and left the other kids at the farm. When we returned to Pensacola, I tried to locate a beach house for rent but they were all taken. At the Marina, I found a large, tri-masted ketch that had been closed up for some time. I called the owner in Ohio. He agreed to come down and rent the boat to Kim and me for the summer. We stored our furniture and most of our household items and moved into our cozy quarters. Jack moved his family into our townhouse and paid the first month's rent. Marty and his wife, Portia, lived near the marina and Kim stayed with them some and babysat their two young children, Eric and Amy. In mid-June, Eric was suddenly stricken with Reyes syndrome. For days, he was comatose and close to death as the infection ravished his body and brain. I offered to sit with him and let Marty and Portia get some rest. While sitting beside his bed and holding his hand, God told me to sing," Jesus loves me." As I sang, Eric began to whistle the tune. It was the first sign that his brain had not been severely damaged and the first sound he had made. As the church continued to pray for Eric, his health was soon restored and it was a joyous experience to see him healed.

My story was published in GUIDEPOSTS magazine that July, and I will never forget the feeling of seeing it in print. It was a good summer. I got out my easel and painted several seascapes, wrote some poetry and enjoyed life. The only cloud that hung over my otherwise, sunny horizon, was Jack Jackson. After the first rent payment he produced a myriad of excuses but very little money. After several months, it was obvious I had made a big mistake. When his house sold, Jack went to Nashville and used the money to cut a record. He bought a new wardrobe for the trip and that left zero dollars for equity on my house. In seven months, I collected less than $400 in rent and eventually had the sheriff evict him and his family. Damages cost over a thousand to fix and I was stupid enough, to once again, believe Mr. Baylor when he said he could get me a quick sale.

It is so difficult for me to disbelieve Christians, when they tell me they will do something. Christians should make every effort to keep their word. Occasionally, we all fall short in keeping our word but some make a habit of it! At the end of the summer, I dropped the full-time curriculum, found a condo on the beach to rent and took a job as machinery designer with St.Regal Paper company. It paid good money and it looked as if I would be able to get out of the financial pit I had dug for myself.

Living on the beach was a delightful experience for me and the kids. We spent many, happy hours, swimming, fishing and exploring, with Pensacola Bay in our backyard and the ocean just across the street from our front door. One day, when I heard hammering coming from the garage basement below, I called down and asked Paul what was going on. He said he was building a sailboat for him and David. I said fine and went back to my business, soon forgetting the incident. A few days later, Paul found me in the kitchen and insisted I come down to the garage. He was obviously excited about something so I left the cooking and followed him and David downstairs. There, stood a five foot sailboat, complete with mast, sail and rudder, on the garage floor. Paul was grinning, quite pleased that he had surprised me. The hull was constructed from a large piece of styrofoam which had floated up on the beach. The mast was a tent pole and the sail was made from old, discarded drapes. The rudder, he had carved from an old, wooden, real estate sign. I was impressed, for I had pictured a tiny, toy sailboat but he had made the real thing, using scraps and ingenuity. The water in the bay behind the condo was shallow for quite a distance out and I allowed the boys to sail their boat there. It was their Robinson Crusoe summer and one they will likely never forget.

In December of that year, I had a strong feeling we should go to Texas and spend Christmas with the folks. I took some vacation time and we packed and headed for home. It was our first Christmas at home since the move to Florida. While there, it began to snow and the kids spent much of their time, playing in the white blanket that covered the ground. Dad watched from the living room window, laughing at their antics. After Christmas, we drove north to Missouri to spend four days with good friends, formerly from Pensacola, Jim and Mary Crews and their family. Six inches of snow covered their small town and the children, mine and theirs, virtually lived outside in it. They built a snowman so fine that his proud picture made the local paper. We hung a string before the fireplace to dry socks and mittens. It was a good trip, though long and tiring, but the decision to go proved to be a wise one. In the spring, a call came from Texas. Dad was in the hospital, critical. He was dying of stomach cancer. The doctor said he might live several months. He was eighty-four and I prayed that God would take him quickly. In two weeks, the call came. He was gone to his home with the father and there would be no more pain. I didn't want the children to remember their granddad, who had loved them so dearly, in a casket. So I left them with a friend and flew home alone for the funeral. It was hard to say goodbye to Daddy. Although we never talked a lot together, we were close. I knew I was a lot like him and when I was young and someone would make me cry or I was hurt, he would bounce me on his knee and sing a silly song until I felt better.

I went in with the family to see Daddy's body lying in the satin lined casket. My older sister, Betty, began to cry aloud. I remember saying, "Don't cry, Daddy's not there in that pile of bones. He's in heaven with Jesus", and I knew it was the truth.

Back in Pensacola, I began to experience headaches, dizziness and nausea on the job. I tried to ignore it at first but the symptoms persisted. One day, with the headache and nausea, came the feeling that I was about to faint. I decided to walk to the nurse's office and have her check me out. I collapsed in front of the desk before I could explain the problem. When I came to, I was in the hospital emergency room and doctors and nurses were there. One doctor said something had caused the oxygen to leave my blood. If the technician in the ambulance had not given me oxygen, I would not be alive. He said it was a very rare and dangerous occurrence. I would have to stay in the hospital until they could determine the cause. It was after two weeks of testing that they discovered hydrogen-sulfide poisoning. There was enough in my system to cause me to drop dead. It was the same gas used for chemical warfare. When dropped on enemy soldiers, once they breathed the gas, the oxygen left their blood and they died almost instantly. Somehow, this strange gas had gotten into my bloodstream. Once there, it might leave the system in a matter of weeks or months but it could reactivate, remove the oxygen from the blood again and kill its' victim. Not a very pretty picture. At the doctor's orders, several people I worked with were tested and found to have minute amounts in their blood but nobody knew why I had a lethal dose.

The doctor would not sign a medical release for me to return to work until the poison left my system. The company, very quietly and unsympathetically, terminated my job while I was hospitalized. I was ineligible for unemployment insurance without a medical release so, I was in a mess. I had no job, no way to get one, no way to support my family. I definitely did not like the feeling of being unable to make the wheels turn that kept my life moving. But as always, in my seemingly, hopeless situation, I turned to God. Soon my mother began to call and ask us to return to Texas. She was lonely and wanted the grandchildren near. I told her to have my sister check around about jobs. It seemed to me a possible solution. If I found a job in my hometown, I could support my children and we would be near family. Joe had long ago left the area to avoid paying child support.

Soon, my sister called, to report that a drafting design job was open at Perry Equipment company. I had worked for them before. She gave me the phone number and I called my former boss. It was mid-May and he said he would hold the job for me until the first of June, after school was finished for the kids. Even though Kim would be in her senior year, she was ready to move back to Texas. She attended Pensacola High School with over a thousand students. It was mid

70's and race riots were a regular event at her school. She wanted to go back to a small, country school. When we first moved to Pensacola, I began a family tradition that proved to be a great help to us all. One evening each week, we would have a family conference. I told the kids how things were going from my viewpoint. I praised them for little individual things they had done the past week that made me happy and told them the things they needed to work on. I tried to be completely honest with them at all times. They in turn, did the same. If I was doing something that bothered or upset them, they told me about it. If they were having problems with each other, it all came out. It was a therapy session that helped us help each other. I was always amazed at the little things, good and bad that were mentioned. I learned how extremely perceptive children are and the deep need they have to be listened to. So when we discussed returning to Texas, the vote was a unanimous yes.

It was a painful move. We left so many close and longtime friends. Pensacola was where we learned to live in freedom. It was the place I discovered the reality of God which had changed my life. It was like leaving a large part of us behind. Kim wanted to finish her senior year at Graford, the little town where I grew up. I rented an old-fashioned house across the street from the school and we settled in. I drove the seventeen miles to work each day and Kim found a summer job at a fast food restaurant in Mineral Wells. Paul got a part-time job with CETA at Graford. The townhouse in Pensacola had still not sold so I was still making mortgage payments. The more I thought about that quick sale, ha, the more I got upset so I tried not to think about it. We were home in Texas and I was working. Things were looking up.

10

Bittersweet Days

In Texas, I couldn't locate a church anything like the one we were a part of in Florida that was near enough for us to attend so I opted not to go anywhere. That was a big mistake. The devil had a heyday with us that year. Christians need other Christians. I didn't even have a close friend. Two girls from my high school graduating class lived in the town but both were married, so I felt isolated and alone. Texas winters where we lived, are generally mild but that year we had week upon week of ice and snow. The old house was uninsulated so the only warm place was a radius of a few feet around the living room space heater or in the bathroom. The boys toughed it out in their cold room at night but the girls and I slept in the living room by the fire. Kim hadn't dated a lot, so when she met a young boy in Mineral Wells, they soon decided they were in love. This didn't bother me a lot until they said they wanted to quit school at midterm and get married! When I told her it was out of the question, she got upset. The boy's parents had no problem with the idea of the kids getting married and said they could come and live at their house. It became a tense situation which I lifted up in prayer. After a few weeks, Kim gave up the idea and even quit seeing the young boy.

Paul was taking Agriculture at school and needed a lamb to raise for a project. In the spring, the lambs would be judged, then sold at auction. Paul's lamb cost eighty-five dollars and we split the cost. There was a barn behind the house where we kept the pretty little ewe that he dubbed, Boots. Every day he fed her, groomed her and exercised her. One morning, a week before the show, he went out to check on her before school. A neighbor's, shepherd dog had chewed a hole through the old, wooden boards and mutilated his pretty Boots. The Ag teacher told him to skin her and dress out the meat so it would not be a total loss. When

I came home from work, I found him cutting up his lamb in the bathtub. There was blood on his face, where he kept wiping away the tears. That was the day my young son became a man. We gave the meat away since none of us had the heart to eat it.

Kim and Heidi wanted a puppy for Christmas and David wanted a goat. I got Heidi a blonde, cocker spaniel puppy and Kim, a toy terrier, Celia. She was the one attacked in a former chapter. I found David a black, baby goat he called Midnight. When Paul would exercise Boots, David would take Midnight walking too. He put a rope around his neck and did more pulling than walking, as the goat had a definite stubborn streak. His fun was short-lived, as one cold, February night, Midnight was climbing in the barn, slipped and caught his head between two boards, hanging himself. We were all very sad but David mourned for weeks. One morning, in February with ice and snow covering the ground, before I went to work, I put down newspapers in the bathroom floor and left the puppies there. When the kids came home from school, smoke was coming out around the bathroom window. Kim called the fire department and kept the other children outside until the truck arrived. They discovered the puppies had somehow knocked over the space heater. Plastic bottles had melted in the medicine chest. The paint had blackened and was bubbling, melting off the walls. The bathroom was virtually destroyed but had not gone up in flames, which was a miracle. They found the puppies safe in the back of the dirty laundry bin, covered with smoke and soot.

During the coldest weather, the twenty houseplants I had carefully carried from Florida, froze in the dining room with the heater on right next door in the living room. In the spring, the house became infested with ticks. They got into the rugs, the sofa and our beds. I had had enough! It had been the worst year we had experienced since we left Texas. After school ended, we would head for the Fort Worth, Dallas, Metroplex and forget the country life.

To top it off, in March a telegram arrived from the real estate agent in Florida, saying the townhouse had been burglarized, vandalized, even ripped up carpets, strongly recommend you sign papers which will arrive soon. Have a buyer to take up payments, no equity. It was signed sincerely, J. Baylor. Discouraged and somewhat overwhelmed, when the papers arrived, I signed them and lost every penny I had invested into the townhouse. Why do some Christians deceive and harm other Christians? No wonder, the world has difficulty seeing Jesus!

In March, I got a letter from my longtime friend, Mary Peres. Mary was an intellectual and it had taken a long time for her to accept the simplicity of Jesus Christ being offered on the cross for our sins. But after a year or so of witnessing, mainly by mail, Mary had recently become a Christian. Her letter said she was going to New York City in June to visit friends that she and her ex-husband had met in Germany. She wanted me to go along. Her friends, Rolph and Toni were also intellectuals and she wanted to share with them about Jesus. Over the years, Rolph had become a heavy drinker because he thought he had committed the unforgivable sin (blasphemed the Holy Ghost) when he was a child. She wanted me to talk to him, since I knew more about the Bible. I wrote back, that I would love to go but thought it would be impossible. I had no vacation time coming and no extra money for the trip. During the following weeks, however, I kept thinking about the trip and felt something inside was urging me to go. I brought the subject up at a Bible study and asked the group to pray with me about it. Later, one of the women from the group, came to me alone and said she felt that God wanted me to go and he had instructed her to provide the money. It seemed an answer to prayer, but I still didn't have any time off, coming. Then it dawned on me. The kids would be out of school in May. Since we were planning a move to the metroplex, I could terminate my job when I left for New York and find one in the metroplex when I returned. Then we could move. After working out the details, I called Mary. I was going to New York after all. I turned in my resignation near the end of May. The kids went to their grandmother's farm and I drove to Atlanta airport to meet Mary. She drove up from south Florida and met me there, where we left my car.

Mary and I had a lot to catch up on as we drove across the states, stopping in Virginia overnight, at the home of her brother and his family. When we arrived in New York City, we found the apartment near Columbia University, where Rolph was studying for his Masters degree. I was overwhelmed by all the iron bars, locks and intercoms we had to pass through just to get inside the apartment. Rolph and Toni's place turned out to be a major meeting place for a hodgepodge of their friends across the nation. Other than ourselves, there were four other visitors. Rolph and Toni were black as were all the other visitors. We arrived late in the afternoon and after unloading our luggage, we all congregated in the kitchen for omelets. After dinner, dishes were cleared away and we migrated to the dining room table where the talk soon turned to religion.

"Mary, I understand you are Christian now," Rolph commented.

"Yes, I am and it's amazing how drastically my life has changed," she replied.

"Changed how?" He asked.

"Well, I'm a different person. I look at everything now in a different way. I read the Bible and understand it for the first time and it seems to have all the answers for my life. I haven't found them all yet but I found a lot of them and it's hard to explain but my life is just not the same anymore. I have a lot more peace."

That was the beginning of an all-night discussion about God, Jesus, the Bible and what it was all about. Mary passed most of the questions over to me and all night long, Mary, myself and the Holy Spirit were on the firing line. Some of the group were earnestly curious, some suspicious, some seeking truth. I knew the Holy Spirit was there because some of the answers that came from my mouth astounded me. Around midnight, Rolph asked me to go to the kitchen to help him with refreshments. It was a ploy to get me alone.

"Jen," he began," I know everything you said in there is true but I can't have it. You see, when I was nine, I blasphemed the Holy Ghost and the Bible says that is the unforgivable sin." When I looked at him, I saw tears moving slowly down his face, glistening in the kitchen light.

"Exactly how did you do it, Rolph?" I asked.

"Well, I had heard the preacher talk about the unforgivable sin. He said it was saying bad things about the Holy Ghost, blasphemy, he called it. One night, when my mother made me go to church when I didn't want to go, I figured I'd show her, so I went out back of the shed and shouted," I blaspheme you Holy Ghost! You hear. I blaspheme you."

I explained to Rolph that it would be quite impossible for a child of nine to blaspheme the Holy Ghost. It comes from adults who profanely curse and continually deny the Holy Spirit. I told him that he was guilty of rebellion but he certainly had not committed the unforgivable sin.

"You mean it! All these years I thought I was condemned to hell but I was wrong."

"That's right. You were wrong. The devil has been lying to you", I replied. He swooped me up and began to swing me around the kitchen until the others came to see what all the laughing and shouting was about. The Bible says in John 8:32," you shall know the truth and the truth shall make you free."

Around daybreak, we all went to bed until noon. Then some of us went sightseeing around the city. After dinner, the group would gather for another session. We discussed a myriad of different things but usually the topic of religion would resurface. This was the schedule we followed, almost unerringly, for a week. One evening, one of the male guests named Clyde, began to get hostile. After it continued a while, God prompted me to ask him why he hated whites. When I asked, he looked shaken, as if I was reading his mail. He became angry and called me a fake. You could feel the tension around the table." You can't speak in any unlearned language! "He challenged. Very quietly and calmly I began to speak in my new language (1 Cor.14:22). The room became as silent as a tomb. When I finished, Clyde simply said, "I'm sorry." His hostility was all gone. The next day, Rolph told me that Clyde was a Black Panther.

I had finished what God had sent me to do so I flew back to Atlanta, picked up my car and went home. Mary stayed another week. I was awed at the way God plans and directs our lives, when we are in tune with his leading. That June, I found a good job in Ft. Worth. It paid more money and I rented a nice apartment just ten minutes from my work in Arlington. Kim was making plans to attend Weatherford Junior College, some thirty miles away and would live there, on campus. Paul was still very uncomfortable around new people and asked to stay on the farm with my mother and drive the twenty odd miles to Graford School, where he would be a Junior. It was a difficult decision. I wanted Paul with the family but I knew he would be miserable in a large, new school and he could be help and company to my mother, who lived alone. I decided to let him stay and it worked out well. Heidi, David and I moved into our new apartment and by fall, were settled in. Heidi was in the ninth grade and attended a junior high school with over 900 students. In the annual, art class contest, Heidi won the honor of" artist of the year". It was obvious that God had blessed her artistically. We attended a church that met in an old, restored warehouse and the people, for the most part, were on fire for God. Speakers from all over came to our church and gave testimonies of what God had done in their lives. One was former Mr. Universe, who had gotten saved, when a little old lady stopped by his table in a restaurant where he had ten different vitamins spread out on the table. She had commented," There is one pill you don't have there, young man."

"What's that?" He asked, puzzled.

"The Gospill", she replied, smiling.

That began the conversation that led him to give his life to Christ. Another time, Reggie Vincento came and told how he was in a motel room with a former state, beauty queen. He said he weighed ninety-five pounds, his hair was very long, his fingernails were painted red and he was totally addicted to drugs and alcohol. Billy Graham appeared on the TV set in the motel room, pointed his finger and said," Jesus wants you!" Reggie fell to the floor, weeping and repenting, surrendering his life to Jesus Christ. When the former beauty queen saw what was happening, she did the same. They called a preacher from the phone book, who came and baptized them in the motel pool. Reggie had been a former rock and roll songwriter for Alice Cooper and Kiss.

It was a real time of growing spiritually for me. I learned from the Bible that the mission of the devil on earth is to kill, steal and destroy (John 10:10) but with Jesus inside us we have the power to resist the devil and he will flee (James4:7). One night, in church, as I listened to a visiting missionary, God spoke to me and said," I will send you to a Spanish speaking country". Later, the message was confirmed to me through other Christians and I accepted it as the will of God. I also had a dream, that God sent me to Mexico and to another far off, Spanish speaking country. When I awoke, I knew the dream had come from God, a night vision, as the Bible calls it.

At church, I met a dedicated man about my age, Tom Craney. His wife had left him, when he gave up a lucrative accounting career and began to build and restore old houses, as God had instructed him to do. We both attended a Friday night Bible study group and soon became close friends. Tom restored a beautiful, old East Dallas mansion and felt God wanted him to use it as a halfway house. He knew I liked working with young people and asked if I would like to be involved in the halfway house. I could live upstairs with my children and be house mother to girls and young women. He would live downstairs and be house dad to boys and young men. His three, young children lived with their mother but would visit him at times. After praying about it, I felt God approved and the children and I moved into the old mansion. Kim soon moved in, after a nasty incident, involving a professor at the college. She found a job at a large, downtown, department store and commuted by bus.

Living there, with the sixteen houseguests, we had in all, for almost a year, was a definite learning experience. Our rules were pretty simple. After three weeks you had to have a job or leave. Jobs were plentiful so unless the young people were extremely lazy, they could find work. There was a midnight curfew, chores assigned, required attendance to morning prayer and Bible study. You had to attend church somewhere on Sunday. No smoking inside was allowed, no drinking alcohol, no drugs and no sex. After employed, we required a fee of twenty dollars a week, to help with the expenses. Tom and I both were working and put much of our income into the project. I sent a weekly check to my mother and son, Paul, but after that, most of my salary went to house expenses as did Tom's. We could see spiritual growth in some, who got their lives together while living there but in others we couldn't. It was a constant battle to get some to do their chores. Some stole food from the kitchen and broke other rules. One month, we paid over $500 for long distance calls, all made by one young lady. In December, one young man intercepted the mail daily, removed the money and checks inside and dropped the empty envelopes behind the clothes dryer. One day, I accidentally walked in on him in the act. He quickly dropped the letter behind the dryer and there we found the other, opened mail. Tom is not easily upset, and I must say he handled it all better than myself. I was shocked and outraged that people would so cruelly use us, when we were doing and giving everything to help them. After several months, we decided we had not seen a lot of fruit from our labor so we prayed and asked God for guidance. We specifically asked, if he wanted the house closed to send a buyer for the house. In only a matter of weeks, a man came by with cash and wanted to buy the house, even though it had not been advertised for sale. We took it as an answer from God and Tom sold the house.

We had some good memories from the old house. Tom played guitar and on Saturday nights, we had a song and praise and study time for anyone who wanted to attend. Some nights, we had twenty to thirty who assembled and sang and prayed until midnight. God did a lot of good things during those meetings. I remember I had a car for sale which I advertised. One day while I was working, someone came by to look at it. He asked if he could drive it around the block. Tom gave him the keys and that was the last we saw of the car. The police said they could not help because we gave the man the keys, which seemed strange to me. Anyhow, we prayed about the car at one of the meetings. A few weeks later, a young man who lived across Dallas said he thought my car was in his apartment, parking lot. We loaded up to go check it out and sure enough, it was there, abandoned with a pink slip from the police on it. We had no key but it was unlocked so the guys hotwired it and we stole it back and drove it home. What a coincidence, ha! Another time, just before Tom sold the house, someone stole our terri-poo, Joshua. He was one of a litter of Celia's pups and his dad was a white, toy poodle. He stayed in our fenced backyard, while I was away at work. One afternoon, he was gone. Since I always prefer things natural, I never had his brown, curly hair clipped, poodle fashion. He was just fuzzy and lovable.

Joshua was very special to our family for God had used him for a mighty miracle that none of us would ever forget. It happened while we lived in a Dallas apartment that required a large, pet deposit. So we left Joshua on the farm with my mother and Paul. School was out for the summer and both my boys were at the farm. On weekends, I would drive down to spend time with Mother and the kids. One such Friday evening, I arrived a little before sundown. Mother was on the front porch. After an exchange of greetings, she said I should check Joshua's eye, because she was afraid the neighbor boy had shot it out with a BB gun. She added that at lunch time, she told my boys to check it but they had gone down in the woods with their cousin, Robbie. When I found Joshua, or rather he found me, his right eye was closed and the eyelid stuck and matted. He couldn't open the eye. I put my hand on his head and said a simple little prayer, asking God to heal the eye. Then, I took him inside to the bathtub, where I bathed him and gently washed away the sticky matter from his wounded eye. When he opened it, everything looked normal and I showed my mother. She said she saw the neighbor boy shooting at Joshua and had made him leave, but was afraid he had shot him in the eye and maybe put it out. Just before dark, my two boys and Robbie came in for supper.

"Hi mom," Paul said." How's everything going?"

"Fine," I replied." Mother said Joshua's eye was hurt and it was a mess, but after I bathed him it looks okay. I guess God healed it when I prayed for him." All three boys reacted as if they had seen a ghost but Paul was the first to respond," What? Where is he?" Seeing the look of shock on their faces I said," what's wrong with you boys? You have seen God heal our dogs before." Acting as if they didn't hear, the three of them tore out the door looking for Joshua. When they came back inside, they were shaking their heads in disbelief and muttering.

"I can't believe it, I just can't believe it," they repeated in turn, over and over.

"Okay, guys, what's going on? You act as if you've seen a ghost. What's going on?" I demanded.

"Mom," Paul said," at lunch, Grandmother told us to check Joshua's eye because she thought Johnny shot it. Well, we did. It was all stuck together but we pulled the eyelid open."

"So," I said.

"What we found was an empty socket. The eyeball was gone!"

"Oh dear God," I said overwhelmed." Are you sure?"

"Were sure, Aunt Jen," said Robbie." It was an empty hole with no eyeball and we all saw it." The miracle was almost more than our earthly minds could handle. None of us had ever seen anything like it and it took a while for the magnitude of it to register.

So naturally, we were all sad when Joshua disappeared from the backyard of the halfway house and had prayed for his return. But, when the day came for us to move, Joshua was still gone. As we were loading our belongings into a borrowed, pickup truck, a funny looking, clipped poodle came up to me and began to whine. I took a moment to pat it on the head and say hello. He had on a rhinestone collar and toenails painted hot pink. When I went inside for another load, the dog followed me and began to scratch at the back of my leg. When I turned to make it go away, I saw the long, curly eyelashes and recognized the face. It was Joshua! I was overjoyed and he rode up front with Kim and me, on our move back to Mineral Wells. Tom moved to Mineola in East Texas, where he later built a house and several cabins. In Mineral Wells, I rented an old building and opened an arts and crafts store-studio with $500 that Tom had given me as a gift, from the sale of the house. I made and sold driftwood and flower creations and gave art lessons. I also got a part time evening job as a reporter for a weekly newspaper. The store was a financial failure so I closed it before a year was up and went back to drafting. One weekend, when I was out of town, I left Joshua with Mother at the farm. A car struck and killed him in her driveway. Our blessed little dog was gone and we all mourned his loss.

11

When You Think You've Got It Together

Paul graduated from high school and found work as a welder's helper in Mineral Wells. I tried to talk him into junior college but he was not to be persuaded. He loved to hunt and fish with his one and only close friend, Sandy DeHaan. They had been buddies for years and usually kept us well stocked with fish or dove or whatever was in season. Paul had an old, yellow Plymouth that broke down regularly, so he got to be pretty good as a mechanic, by taking it apart and fixing it. Everything he learned he would teach David, if he could get him still, long enough. It always amazed me, how much the boys learned about man stuff, hunting, cars, etc., without a father to teach them. Thinking it might be a long, long time before God allowed me to go to the mission field, I bought a two acre, plot of land that was covered with trees and had a little creek at the back. It was located just south of Mineral Wells. I didn't take the time to pray about it but just decided that I was tired of moving from pillar to post and wanted a real home for the family. My dad had been a part-time carpenter and Paul had worked some as a carpenter's helper, so I figured, with the kids help, I could build us a little house in the woods. I would work and pay for the supplies, as we built. Kim and Heidi had an apartment in town and Paul was still living with my mother on the farm so David and I moved into the apartment with the girls. I drew up a simple set of house plans and ordered the first load of lumber.

It wasn't quite as simple as I had hoped. Kim helped me clear the spot we had picked for the house, which was to be pier and beam foundation, located on the side of a sloping hill. The whole family came out for a weekend and worked diligently, clearing briars and brush for a driveway and getting everything ready. Two weeks later, after much more hard work, a neighbor lady stopped by and informed me that we had cleared her brothers' land. The man from the development had shown me the wrong piece of land. I had bought the plot next door. After the mess was straightened out, I moved over, found another house site and began again. The family was not so anxious to come out and help the second time. Before I began the main house, Paul helped me build a one-room cabin on the corner of the land, where David and I would live, while building the house. After we settled, I built and leveled the foundation for the house. The plan was to underpin with sandstone and mortar. Sandstone was abundant on the two acre plot. David's job was to carry the rocks to the house site, where I cemented them into place. At one point, when I went down the hill to check on David's long, overdue return, I found he had tied a large rock on the end of a rope and the opposite end was tied to our Irish setter. He was trying to convince the dog to pull the rock uphill to the house site. The prospect of carrying rocks did not appeal to David in the least and I spent much of my time, trying to keep him on the job. One day, when I was nailing some of the last boards onto the subfloor, I stopped for a short break and heard God's voice say, "it's time now, Jen."

"Time for what?" I asked.

"Time to go to Spanish school and the mission field," he replied.

"No, God, this can't be you talking. I've just started this house, you see, and I can't leave it unfinished. It's just not a good time to go and I won't believe this is you, unless you prove it to me." When I say I heard God's voice, I mean inside my head, not in my ear, but it was just as clear and real as if it had been audible.

For several months, I had been owed money for work I had done for an oil company. Despite a number of calls, they still had not paid me.

"The money from the oil company will arrive in the morning," I heard the voice say.

And a well-known, Christian singer is coming home to heaven this week."

"Well, God, if these two things come to pass I will know it's you talking, and I will pack my bags. But, what about the house?"

"Leave the house to me." And that was the end of the conversation. The next morning, when I checked with the oil company, the secretary said that my check had arrived in the mail that morning, from the main office. Two days later, Keith Green's plane crashed and he indeed, went home to heaven. Of all the Christian singers, there was something about Keith's music, the words of his songs, that touched me more than any other. I knew about a Spanish school at McAllen, on the border. It was called Kings Way Missionary Institute and taught Spanish and missionary ethics, to prospective missionaries. I called them and requested an application form. When I returned it, I was accepted for classes which would begin in ten days. I felt God said to leave, on the following Wednesday. There was just one, little problem. Most of the check, I had picked up from the oil company, I had spent on land payments and utilities. I had a grand sum of ten dollars, left over. The money that I had made lately, had gone to buy supplies to build the house. I knew if God wanted me to go, he would somehow provide the money but I was a bit anxious, to say the least. As I made preparations to leave, I kept feeling an urge to call Kim and ask her to go with me. The urge wouldn't go away.

Kim had given her life to Christ in her early teens but I knew that she had recently returned to Dallas and was not following God. I didn't really think she would leave her job at International Wildlife Park and her Marine boyfriend, Jonny, to go to Spanish school with me. But, I had learned not to ignore those persistent urges. It was usually the Holy Spirit trying to lead me, so I called Kim. I told her that God had confirmed it was time for me to go to Kings Way. We talked for a few minutes and I shared some of the things that had been happening.

"Why don't you come with me?" I suggested.

"I just might do that," she replied." I'll call and let you know in a couple of days." I was surprised but realized that it might be God. Two days later, she called to say she had contacted the Spanish school and they told her, she could enroll. She would come to McAllen in about a week, as she had to give a weeks notice before leaving her job.

On Tuesday, I packed my old van with some of mine and David's belongings. I still had only ten dollars. That evening, we went to a revival meeting that was in progress at the little church we attended. Everything had happened so fast, I hadn't told anyone, except family, that David and I were leaving. That evening at church, I shared a bit about what God had instructed me to do. I was careful not to mention that I didn't even have the gas money for the trip. When the collection plate had been passed earlier, I dropped in our last ten dollars. After I had shared with the congregation our plans, one of the elders suggested that they pass the offering plate again, just for David and me. Usually, the offering at our little church was thirty to fifty dollars. The revival had been going on for several weeks and the offering was collected nightly, so the people had very little to give. God did a miracle and our basket contained more than three hundred dollars. If I had any lingering doubts about God being behind this venture, they vanished that night. Early, the next morning, we said a tearful goodbye to the family and headed out with mother's last, cheerful words," don't get yourselves killed!"

The eleven hour trip to McAllen was uneventful. We arrived at Kings Way around five that afternoon. Don Russell, the school president, met us in the office, with a warm smile. Dinner was being served in the cafeteria so he showed us where to freshen up, then took us over and introduced us to several people. Over our meal, we got to know a few people casually. After dinner, we were shown the available choices of housing. I chose a late model, twenty-eight foot, travel trailer with one bedroom, which Kim and I could share, and a sofa bed for David. It had a modern, little kitchen and tiny bath. The rent was one hundred a month, as was the tuition. Water was furnished and on Thursday, I made an electric deposit, filled the two, five gallon, propane bottles and spent thirty dollars on food and supplies. We were now, back down to ten dollars.

I registered David at middle school about a mile from campus and Kim arrived the following week in her old, Ford car and with five hundred dollars. We soon settled into our new lifestyle at the school. The environment was like nothing I had experienced before. All of the students and staff were Christians and many of them, baptized in the Holy Spirit. Nearly always, outside of class, people got together and prayed for one another or the school or whatever and in the evenings you could find a group with a guitar, singing, talking and praising the Lord. Sometimes in class, we prayed, sang and worshiped, instead of studying. All of the people were human and on occasion, whiny, petty or grumpy, but the atmosphere of love was overwhelming.

After a couple of months, when Kim's money was depleted, we decided to sell her old car. We only needed one vehicle and my van was handy to haul a large load of students to Padre Island, once a month for a picnic and a break from classes. We agreed six hundred would be a fair price for her car and advertised it, put a notice on the bulletin board and passed the word around campus. But for all our efforts, nothing happened. We had absolutely zero response. I began to get a bit uptight. Our tuition would be due in a few days, our rent was almost due and our electric bill was past due. Not only that, but each time I prayed about selling the car, God would say, "I want you to give the car to Steve." Steve was a fellow student and we liked him but I was afraid to tell Kim what God was saying to me. We needed that money, and besides, it was her car. Secretly, I hoped the message wasn't coming from God at all. Then one day, Kim brought the subject up.

"Mom, I'm beginning to wonder about that car," she said.

"Yeah," I agreed." It's sure not selling very fast, is it?"

"Actually," she continued," every time I pray about it, I feel God is telling me…"

"To give it to Steve," I interrupted.

"How did you know?" She asked.

"Because he told me the same thing but I was afraid to tell you."

"Well," she laughed," I guess that's confirmation enough. Let's go find Steve." We found him at home in the pickup, camper shell, where he lived. When we told him God had instructed us to give him the car, tears welled up in his eyes. He shared with us how he had been praying for a car. He had come to Kings Way with a wife, a new car and a pickup truck. He planned to sell one of the vehicles for tuition and rent. He and his wife were living in one of the apartments there but two weeks after arriving, she called an old boyfriend to meet her and they left together in the new car. A few days later, they got greedy, slipped back in the middle of the night and stole the pickup truck. When his rent came due and he didn't have it, someone gave him the pickup camper to live in and now, he also had a car. Kim and I learned that God will lead us by his Spirit if we will listen and obey. The next day, a man approached me after morning worship and slipped something into my hand.

"God said to give you this for rent." He said, smiling. When I looked, it was a hundred dollar bill. How did he know the amount of our rent? God had told him of course! This was a mind-boggling new way of life for us. Many of the people were walking, living, and moving in the spirit. I had read about it happening in the underground church in communist countries but never in my life, had I seen it in action and now I was in the middle of it!

Now we had rent money but there was still the matter of tuition and the electric bill. The refrigerator and kitchen cabinets were all but empty, too. I began to pray in earnest and God said to trust him and not tell anyone, so that is what I did. I told Kim and David not to mention our need to anyone, that God would handle it his way. In a couple of days, when the electric company came to disconnect our meter, I felt sad but with an effort, I made myself sing and praise the Lord. When Kim and David came home, Kim joined in but David thought it foolish to sing and praise God with our electric cut off and no food in the house. After dark, our neighbor came over.

"Y'all sound happy," she said." Is something wrong with your electricity?"

"Well sort of," I replied.

"I'll send John over to fix it," she continued.

"I don't think he can," I answered.

"Well you have to fix it. Your food will spoil in the refrigerator." At that we all laughed.

"There's not any food in the refrigerator, Dolly."

"No," she said as she opened the door to look for herself."

"You're out of food and your electric has been shut off. Why didn't you tell us?" She asked, puzzled." You have to have food and electricity."

"I know," I said," but God just said to keep quiet and to praise him."

"Well, I'll be back in a little bit," she said as she went out into the dark.

Our secret was out. Within an hour, people began knocking on the door. Some brought food, some brought money. There was a long stream of visitors, more than willing to share in our time of need. Our cabinets once again were bulging with food and the money was enough to reconnect the electric and pay tuitions, with some left over to supply the refrigerator. David learned that it wasn't foolish to praise God in times of trouble, after all.

Kim's studies came easy and her grades were at the top of the class. For me, my brain was out of practice at studying and all the Spanish had trouble taking root in my computer. Kim made "A's" with a minimum of effort. I made some "A's," but mostly "B's" and an occasional "C" with intense effort. A strange but wonderful thing happened about six weeks into the semester. Kim and I had been praying for her friend, Jonny, in Dallas. One evening, he called and was very upset. God had appeared to him in his dreams, telling him to repent and accept Christ as Savior or he would soon die and go to hell.

"How do I get saved?" He asked. Kim was more than willing to explain how and she led him in prayer on the phone. He asked Jesus into his life. She told him to go to his uncle, who was a preacher, and get baptized. He followed her instructions and a tough Marine began his life for God. The dream was an approach I hadn't heard before but it had worked. I don't care how God gets them when we pray, just so he gets them.

I'm convinced we should make souls a top, prayer priority. Our faith continued to grow in leaps and bounds. One evening, David came hobbling into the house, crying that he had broken his ankle while playing basketball. David was not one to cry easily so I knew he was hurting and there was a large knot protruding from the side of his ankle. We had no insurance and no money for doctors but we had plenty of faith. Kim and I laid hands gently(for he squealed like a pig when we touched it) and we began to pray for God to heal his ankle. Within a few minutes, David stopped crying and began laughing hysterically. He rolled on the floor, convulsing with laughter. Kim and I laughed, too. It was infectious. After several minutes, when we all got back to normal, we checked his ankle and the hard knot had disappeared, along with the pain. Psalms 103:3 says", he is our God who heals all our diseases and forgives all our iniquities. That evening, he healed broken bones as well. Praise the Lord!

The Kings Way curriculum, consisted basically of Spanish with one class on missionary ethics. The courses were college accredited, a four year course crammed into two semesters. We had over four hours of class and two or three hours of homework, five days a week. It was an arduous load for me and without God's daily help, I don't think I could've handled it. One thing bothered me about the teaching at the school. We were regularly reminded that it was virtually impossible for a single woman to survive on the mission field, alone. Young girls were advised to wait until they married and older women were advised to join a group. I didn't know any group and I didn't have any marriage plans, so it was like a fish bone in my craw and I would have to find a solution.

Meanwhile, Kim was happy and growing in the Lord. David was doing well in school and had several friends. The clean, healthy atmosphere of campus life was good for him. He seemed happy and well adjusted. Several of the men on campus, sort of adopted him and helped fill in for the father he never had. Heidi wrote regularly, usually sending five or ten dollars. She was working at a jewelry store and she and her boyfriend, Terry, were still in love. Once, we got a letter from Paul with fifty dollars inside. He said he was working on the house in his spare time. I was touched that Paul was spending his time and money on our unfinished house. God was keeping his promise. Classes for the first semester ended in December. In the first semester, you learned basics. The second semester was advanced Spanish and practical application. At Christmas, Kim chose to stay on campus but David and I went home to Mineral Wells. About a year earlier, I had worked briefly with a man named James, at a home for problem teenagers. We were both counselors. James was a determined sort, and had kept trying to get me to date him. At first, I resisted. But eventually, I dated him a few times. When I discovered that he smoked pot, among other things, I made it clear that I wanted nothing more to do with him. After a while, he left me alone. When I went home that Christmas, I ran into James. He said he had become a Christian and was renting a house in the country. I didn't believe him at first, but after a couple of other people said he seemed to have changed and had his act together, I thought it might be true.

James kept calling my mother's house, where David and I were staying, and kept asking me out. Finally, I agreed to go to dinner with him. When I told him about Kings Way, he said it sounded great. Then he said he thought he would like to get involved in mission work. That surprised me. He sure sounded different! He went on to say that he thought he was in love with me and wanted to marry me. That floored me! For some insane reason, I told him I would think about it. I couldn't forget the old James but maybe he really had changed. People said he had changed. He said he wanted to work in missions. I had been warned that women should not go alone to the mission field. I decided to talk to the pastor and ask him about James. Our pastor said that James seemed to really be living a Christian life. So, after James kept pressing me for an answer, I made one of the biggest mistakes of my life. I told him I would marry him, if we did it within a week, before I changed my mind. I had been single for ten years and something inside of me suggested that James was not Mr. Right. I can never explain, why after waiting so long and being so careful, I suddenly decided to marry James. It was a set up by the devil himself. He dangled a bauble in front of my eyes and I reached out and grabbed it. Somehow, I thought it would be an answer for the mission field. I knew, never to act in haste, to wait upon the Lord, but I allowed that shiny bauble to dazzle me. It was all a lie. James had fooled everyone.

The week we married, he confessed he had lost his job two weeks earlier. His car was borrowed and we were evicted from his place because he hadn't paid rent in several months. After two weeks, I discovered the reason. He was still using drugs regularly. He even tried to get me to borrow money for his habit. People came to our door to get the money they had loaned him. James had a sunny personality and could talk most anyone to loaning him money but he failed to pay it back. I took some odd jobs, and began to pray in earnest about the mess I was in. When I prayed, I felt that God was saying James was married to someone else. After that happened several times, I asked James about it. He said he had been married twice but was legally divorced. When I asked to see the papers, he couldn't produce them. When I decided to pursue the matter, I learned that he had married three women before me and only divorced two of them. His legal wife even called me on the phone! He was a bigamist and our marriage was illegal. It was one of the lowest points of my life. How could I have been so hasty and made such a stupid mistake? At a time in my life, when I seemed to have it all together, had dedicated my life to serving God, I had blown it big time

I went out to my cabin on the land and locked myself inside. I began to repent and weep before the Lord. I fasted and prayed and cried for three days. I had no water and was sick with headache, fever and nausea but it didn't bother me half as much as the feeling of failure that overwhelmed me. At the end of three days, I loaded my clothes into the van, located David with a friend's family so he could finish the school year he had started at mid-term. I told the family goodbye and went back to McAllen. I took a job as a waitress, where Kim was working part-time and moved into a camper trailer, on the outskirts of town. Once again, I turned to God for direction and it was soon on the way.

12

A Parrot Named Regalito

John and Lottie Hall, some friends from Kings Way, who had graduated in December, and moved to central Mexico, invited me down for a visit. I left the van with Kim and took the bus to Valles, San Luis Potosi, where they lived. Their casa was a nice, new, two-story, orange stucco and they gave me a room upstairs. John and Lottie's ministry consisted of Friday night meetings for area, young people and trips into the country villages, usually on Saturday nights, where they showed Spanish versions of the movies such as "The Cross and the Switchblade". John played guitar and set up and operated the equipment and Lottie preached, following the movies. I went along on most of their trips and helped however I could. I promptly got dysentery, accompanied by nauseous headaches from the city's air pollution, so many of my days were spent upstairs in my bed very near the bathroom! It was a time of learning and growing for me. John and Lottie had a large library of Christian books which I devoured while lying in the bed and in my spare time when not convalescing. I chose to read the biographies of Christian men and women who had accomplished a lot during their lifetimes. I read about Dwight Moody, Kathryn Khulman, Hudson Taylor, who opened up the missions to inner China. I read about William Tyndale, the Bible smuggler, George Mueller, the orphanage builder in England and many others. I found them all to be very normal human beings, all with weaknesses and failures but among their lives, I discovered the one, common thread I was searching for. They simply trusted wholeheartedly in God. They believed the promises in his Word were true and they lived those promises and most of them sacrificed their own well-being in exchange for the souls and lives of others. God took these willing, humble, ordinary people and used them greatly as his instruments.

After visiting for a month, I felt the need to shut myself up in my room and fast and pray for God's next step in my life. John and Lottie wanted me to stay and work with them but I knew that God had other plans. So, shutting myself in, with only water, I began to seek the Lord. On the third day, while praying with my eyes closed, a picture came into my mind. I saw a large, whitewashed building in the distance with an ocean in the background and small, brown children, scattered about playing. I knew it was an orphanage. When I heard a voice say, inside of me," this orphanage is where I want you to work for me," I quickly opened my eyes. This couldn't be God, I thought. I had never considered working in an orphanage. Mother said I would go crazy from too much religion. Perhaps I had gone too long without food and I was hallucinating. Mind you, I had purposely shut myself in and denied myself food in an effort to hear from God and when he spoke, I did not believe it was him! Nevertheless, I decided, just in case, on the merest chance that it could be him, to pursue the conversation.

"Okay, God," I said," if this is you, where is the orphanage?" The answer was not what I expected.

"Where you go, you will find a parrot." Now I was sure I had lost it all, but I wasn't going to stop there. My curiosity was aroused.

"Okay, God, if this is you, what color will the parrot be?" I figured if Gideon could send out that fleece the second time, just to be sure, I could ask God the color of the parrot.

"It will be green and red and it will be a gift," was the reply.

After thinking about this unusual conversation for a few moments, I said," okay, God, I will make a deal. If I find a green and red parrot that is a gift, I will start looking for the orphanage." When I went downstairs and told John and Lottie what I thought I heard from God, relating the experience, they didn't seem impressed. They even looked as if perhaps, they agreed with my mother!

I decided to return to Mineral Wells to visit my children while I waited for my passport and further instructions from the Lord. When I checked the bus schedule I noticed that the bus passed through Tampico, Tamualipas. Hank and Krista Webber, some missionaries that I had met once in Dallas and had been corresponding with for the past two years, lived there. I decided to stop off in Tampico and look them up. When I finally found their house, it was enormous and looked more like a mayor's house than a missionary's. When I rang the doorbell, I thought I was hearing things when I heard a parrot say, "hello". Krista answered the door and looked puzzled when I said," hi, I'm Jen Jireh. May I see your parrot?"

"Oh, Jen Jireh. It's good to see you, come on in. You want to see the parrot?" She said, with a strange look on her face. When she led me to the garage, there, perched on top of his cage, was a large, green parrot with red wing tips and a patch of red on his head.

"Oh, it was really God ! Praise the Lord, it was really God." I kept repeating. I kept staring at the bird and Krista kept staring at me." What's his name?" I asked.

"Regalito," she replied." He was a gift to us from friends." In Spanish, regalito means, little gift. I was overwhelmed.

When we went into the kitchen for iced tea, I explained my excitement over the parrot, telling Krista the story of the vision and God's message." That's nice," said Krista," but you must be mistaken, because the only orphanage here is a big, Catholic one, downtown and it is run by nuns.

"There is an orphanage here," I said determinedly," where God wants me to work and he will show it to me."

"Well, we've been here three years and if there was another orphanage, I think we would know about it." Krista's unencouraging words didn't sway me. I knew God had given me the vision and he had led me to the parrot and he would lead me to the orphanage. I stayed the night and met Hank, who also thought I had missed God. In the morning, I headed for the Texas border. Kim's spring graduation was just two days away so I stopped in McAllen to attend it. Heidi flew down and we had a happy, mother-daughter reunion, catching up on what had been happening in all our lives. We packed Kim's belongings into the van, after graduation, and went home to Mineral Wells the following day. I looked up David at the friend's house, where he had been living since February. When I told him about the vision and all that it happened, he agreed to move to Tampico with me and take school by correspondence in the fall. The course was especially designed for missionary kids and cost six hundred dollars. I took a temporary job to raise the money. When July rolled around, Kim was working and decided to stay in Mineral Wells where she was living with Heidi. I had spent the past couple of months, camping out in my cabin and working on the house in my spare time. Paul had completed the plumbing and the fireplace.

I knew if I had taken a poll of my family and a few of my friends that summer, the general consensus would have been that I had some loose screws and maybe lost a few marbles. I had started to build a house with no extra money and now I was heading off into Mexico, with my teenage son, to find an orphanage because I had found a parrot! I had to admit, that to most, it would seem strange, even crazy but the children and a few Christian friends understood.

Ten years before, I believed in God but I didn't know him as a loving father. I believed that Jesus was the way to God, that he died for me on the cross but I thought he lived up in heaven, only. I had no idea, he could actually live inside of me in the person of the Holy Spirit, talk to me, lead and guide me, open up the word to me so that it became real and alive. I knew there was a devil but I thought he lived in hell, never suspecting that he roamed around the earth with his demons to kill, steal, and destroy. And I certainly never knew that I had power through Jesus Christ, living in me, to resist the devil and make him flee, whenever he attacked. I had believed in angels but thought they resided in heaven with God. I had no inkling that whenever I prayed, God could and would send them to fight the devil and his demons and deliver me. I guess what had happened in the past ten years, was I had been in school and God had been my teacher. I was a hardheaded and usually apprehensive student but I had been willing to allow God to teach and change me and that's all that he required. I would continue to be in God's school and hopefully, continue to grow but the first ten years were the most dramatic and had brought the greatest and most difficult changes.

So only those who had come to take God's word, the Bible, literally and live it wholeheartedly, could understand my behavior. If you don't believe in miracles, you probably won't get any. I had believed and seen and experienced them. I would never go back to living my life the way I chose, I wanted, I planned. I would always seek to find the way he chose. He created me and left an instruction manual, the Bible, for me to live by. He saved me and filled me with his spirit to help me live this life.

About dusk, we pulled into the outskirts of Tampico. David came out from under his hat. Suddenly, a bus came at us in our lane. It was passing a car and he seemed to know he was bigger than our van. I took to the ditch to avoid a collision. I was soon to learn, that this is normal driving in Mexico. The right of way goes to whoever gets there first.

"Looks like a big place," David commented, as he took in the sights.

"Tampico and the outlying area have about six million people," I said. David expressed surprise as this was his first trip to Tampico. Somehow, I remembered the way to the Webster's house, where we would be staying until we got located, permanently. Finding my way around has never been one of my strong points. Anyone who knows me will attest to that fact but this time I amazed myself and made all the right turns. Their daughter, Tammy, greeted us at the door. She led us into the kitchen where Krista was helping the maid prepare the evening meal. David and I sat at the kitchen table and drank iced tea with lime, while they continued their preparations. We all chatted about the trip and the iced tea was delicious after the long, hot ride since our last, refreshment stop. Later, Hank came in and we adjourned to the large, dining room for dinner.

After dinner, I told them I believed I knew where David and I were going to live. Some missionaries had visited our church in Mineral Wells about a year earlier. They told of a little house they saw in Tampico, that was empty. It had two stories with two rooms and bath upstairs and two rooms and bath below. They said it needed a lot of paint and fixing but the rent was only forty dollars. It was in the most exclusive part of town. Hank and Krista laughed.

"Jen," said Krista," there are no houses that rent for forty dollars in the best part of town. It's more like four hundred dollars."

"Well, I believe God told me that house was to be mine and David's. Tomorrow, I will look for it." They made an effort to humor me.

"Well, we have a friend who knows his way around. He will be here tomorrow and we will ask him," Hank said, still smiling.

As I lay in bed that night, tired as I was, the dozens of thoughts whirling around in my head, kept me awake into the wee hours. Could I be wrong about the house? And if so, where would we live? And would David adjust and be happy here? I knew that getting him to spend several hours each day on his schoolwork would be a major chore. Maybe Mother was right. Oh, why was it always so difficult to trust God in the middle of the night when you're all alone with your thoughts? In the morning, their friend, Ramon, arrived. He was tall and handsome with a radiating personality. David and I liked him immediately. Later, he and his wife, Marta, would become our closest and dearest friends in Tampico.

After introducing us, Krista smiled and said," Ramon, Jen thinks God told her to rent a little house that's two stories and in the best part of town for forty dollars a month. I told her it doesn't exist but you should know. What do you think?" Ramon rubbed his chin and thought for a moment, then replied," oh yes, I know just where it is." At that point, Krista's mouth fell open and Hank's face took on a startled look.

When Krista found her voice again she said," you do?", in obvious amazement.

"Yes, I believe it is right across the street from Senator Herrera. It sets back in the trees a bit. It's been vacant for several years," he said, speaking good English but with a heavy accent.

"Well, let's go ask around and see if we can locate the owner," said Hank. I got the feeling they were anxious to relocate this strange lady who talks to God about houses and parrots. We found the little house just where Ramon had remembered it. It was just as I had pictured it. Nestled back in the trees between two, giant casas, it stood, looking badly in need of some tender, loving care. The screens had holes that needed mending. The steps were crumbling and needed some cement patching. The blue plaster exterior needed a good scrubbing and all of the interior needed a fresh coat of paint. Under the dirt and silt on the floors, was nice terrazzo tile. The tiny kitchen was lacking cabinets and the bedrooms had no closets but it could be fixed up really nice and I loved it. When we found the owner, she said it rented for forty-two American dollars a month. She added that she would call when she had a lease ready for us. That afternoon, we went to the beach and relaxed in the water and sunshine. The doubts and fears of the night before, seemed to melt away and I was excited about our new life in Mexico. I thought about the orphanage God had waiting for us and wondered when he would show us where it was. One thing at a time, I told myself. God's timing is perfect and when the time is right, he will reveal the orphanage. I thought about my Spanish and wondered if it was good enough to communicate with the people there. Hank and Krista spoke the language fluently and I knew it would take time for mine to be anywhere near that good. Also, I could speak it but what I heard, if it came too rapidly, I couldn't understand it all.

My thoughts were crudely interrupted when David dumped a paper cup of water on my head and took off in a run. I couldn't let that go unanswered so I hastily pursued. It was some three weeks before we could move into our little casa. Getting the electric wiring checked, repaired and approved was time-consuming. I quickly learned that nothing gets done in a hurry in Mexico! David and I went over daily to work on the house or yard. We shoveled out dirt and silt that had washed in during a flood, chased out giant spiders that had taken up residence and rebuilt the front steps. We were a curiosity to the neighbors who soon came over to meet us. We welcomed moving day when it finally arrived. Hank and Krista were gracious hostesses but we were anxious to be in our own, little casa. I made curtains, by hand, from a set of sheets. We had a styrofoam ice chest for a refrigerator and a hot plate for a cook stove. I stacked pieces of lumber on cinderblocks, for cabinets. An old door, put on top of more cinderblocks became our dining table. And two, five gallon paint buckets, turned upside down, became our chairs. I made a closet for each bedroom by hanging pieces of plastic pipe for rods and more sheets providing curtains for them. Our sleeping bags became our beds and so it was that we began our new life in Mexico in our quaint, little, forty dollar house.

We soon developed a routine of sorts. In the mornings, I would make breakfast of taquitos with eggs and peppers on our little grill, clean the kitchen and go upstairs to pray and study the Bible. David would do his lessons downstairs. Before noon, I would do the laundry by hand in our cement sink outside, underneath the trees. Getting it dry was usually a problem with daily showers and high humidity. Sometimes, the clothes would sour before they would dry and I would have to wash them again. Limeade, made with limes from our own trees, became our primary drink. When we tired of it, David would go to the corner tienda for apple flavored sodas that cost eleven cents. On Thursdays, I usually shopped at the mobile mercado that came to our section of town. It was a train of little wagons with bright pink and white, striped canopies. A street would be blocked off and the little wagons were lined up along both sides, each offering different wares. Wagon merchants usually brought their families. The elderly sat around in chairs while the children ran raucously, through the crowds, playing games. I bought vegetables and fruit for the week. Meat was expensive and you never knew what kind of meat you were buying so I skipped it except for an occasional chicken. Our friend, Ramon, took David fishing regularly so we had fresh fish often and sometimes ate meat tacos, downtown.

I had developed the habit of talking out loud to God while working around the house. David thought it was weird but adjusted to my strange conversations with God. Every day, I would say," thank you God for showing us the orphanage. I know you will reveal it when you're ready. I'm not complaining Lord, but we have been in this house three weeks and it is fixed up now. It would be nice to go to work so if you would show it to us soon, I would appreciate it." One day, David listened to me and then said," oh mom, everybody has told you there is no orphanage here except the Catholic one. Why don't you just admit it? There's no other orphanage!"

"There is an orphanage, David. God told me where I found a green and red parrot I would find the orphanage. I found the parrot and I will find the orphanage."

David shrugged his shoulders and replied," okay, there's an orphanage but I won't believe it 'till I see it."

That afternoon, we had visitors, a local preacher named Francis whom we knew, and a stranger, who Brother Francis introduced as Brother Felipe. Over coffee, Francis told us that brother Felipe needed to go far into the country the next evening to preach at a little village but had no car and the bus didn't pass that way. Francis's car was broken and he asked if we would carry brother Felipe in our van. I told him that we would. They left a map to brother Felipe's house and then departed. During breakfast, the next morning, David told me of a strange dream he had in the night." I saw a house on a hill. It was like a small castle, with turrets and all. I could see the ocean behind it. You and I were outside with some children. Must have been an orphanage, huh?" I agreed it was a strange dream and maybe it was an orphanage but had to admit I had no idea what the dream meant, if anything. That afternoon, we took our map and headed for Felipe's house. After making several turns, we found ourselves on a road that ran alongside the beach. Suddenly, David shouted," Mom, look on that hill!" What I saw gave me goose bumps. High on the hill, with the ocean in the background, was a miniature castle.

"That's it, just like the dream," David said, excitedly." Can we stop?"

"I guess, for a moment," I said as I drove up the hill, bewildered. What did it mean? David had seen it in a dream and here it was. Could it be the orphanage? No one was around and the doors were locked so we left and continued to Felipe's. I promised David we would check it out later. After picking up Felipe, I described the building and asked if he knew who owned it.

"Oh yes, the leetle castle, they call hem the Pharaoh 'caus he builds leetle castles. He is very reech and important, "Felipe said in broken English with a heavy accent. When I asked if he knew what that building was used for, he replied, I theenk it is an orphanage."

"Wow," was David's only response. I felt tears on my face. God had given David the dream to increase his faith. He sent Felipe to us so we would go down that road and find it. He had led us to the parrot and now, to the orphanage. I was speechless. Learning to seek God's leading, then wait and watch for it, was still pretty new to me and I found it almost impossible to comprehend.

When we returned to the castle, later in the week and found no one around, a neighbor lady saw us and came over. She didn't speak English so we conversed in Spanish. I asked about the house, if she knew the owner and if it was really an orphanage. She told me that she had seen the owner only a few times. He was very rich and important and was called the Pharaoh. Yes, it was an orphanage but the orphans had been moved down closer to the water in another house. She pointed to a road that disappeared into a grove of trees. When I asked if the other house was built like a castle, she replied, "oh yes, all of them are." David and I walked down the road to the orphanage. Sure enough, it looked like another little castle. Six curious orphans came outside. When I asked for the manager (jefe), they ran ahead of us inside, shouting.

"Magdalena, someone is here to see you." Magdalena remained seated in front of the television when David and I entered the room. The children circled around us, wide eyed and quiet. Fair haired gringos are rare that far south in Mexico and we were probably the first they had seen, close up. I introduced myself and explained in Spanish that I was interested in working there.

"Oh no, there is no money for workers. I come two hours a day and that is all. There is no more money." When I said I didn't want money, only to work with the children, she looked at me as if I was joking." No money, you want to work in this place for free?" I told her God had sent me and David and we only wanted to help the children, however we could. I asked about the owner, the Pharaoh. She said I couldn't see him because he was too busy and important but she agreed to ask if we could work there for free. When we returned in a week, Magdalena said the Pharaoh said it would be okay. I could tell that she felt threatened about me taking her job. Maybe she hadn't even talked to the Pharaoh, but it didn't matter. All that mattered was that we were allowed to work with the orphans. We had found the orphanage that everyone said didn't exist. What's more, we knew it was God who led us there, just like in the Bible with dreams and visions.

13

Wedding Bells and Angels

David and I began going to the orphanage every afternoon right after lunch. It was a large, modern building, with beds for sixty children. I asked Magdalena why there were only six children living there. She told me the Pharaoh said it cost too much to keep them and never allowed more than a few. I had never met this Pharaoh and already I didn't like him. Magdalena would usually leave when we arrived each day. She cooked lunch for the kids and then watched TV until her two hours were up. The rest of the day and night the children were unattended. José Luis was fifteen and the oldest. He took care of the younger ones. Juan was ten, Raul was nine, Jaime and Arturo were seven and Martin was five. Magdalena was a bit lazy and the place and the children were filthy. The boys had lice and no toothbrushes or soap. I brought soap, toothbrushes and toothpaste, shampoo and a solution to kill the lice. After teaching the boys some basic hygiene, I started cleaning the orphanage. I told the boys if they would help me clean for one hour each day, I would buy them a basketball and baseball equipment. They agreed it would be a fair trade and pitched in to help. The kitchen looked as if it had never been cleaned. Cockroaches were everywhere, even in the refrigerator. It took weeks just to clean the kitchen. I kept my bargain and after helping me clean each day, the boys played ball with David. Sometimes, we would go to the beach and after getting permission from Magdalena, we took the boys on excursions to the ship docks or to a movie. After we got the place cleaned, we used our cleaning time for Bible studies. The boys were eager to listen and soon began to tell their favorite Bible stories to us. We gave them all Spanish Bibles and taught them some Scriptures and a few songs in Spanish.

The promised support from our church back home was used instead, for a building program, so much of my prayer time was used in praying for our daily needs. God had told me never to ask for support from others so we basically depended on him. Kim and Heidi sent a small amount around the first of the month and Paul sent larger amounts but less often. Our average income in Tampico was sixty-five dollars a month but with God's help, we made it! A couple of months after we moved into our little casa, one evening we were returning home from the orphanage and I noticed the alternate gas tank on the van read empty. The main tank had been empty for weeks. When we went inside to prepare dinner, I also noticed the food was all but gone. The next day was shopping day but I remembered I had no money. I had been so busy lately, I had failed to notice that the regular letters from Kim and Heidi had not arrived. Fear suddenly gripped my insides. We were out of money, food and gas! I prepared tortillas and heated the last of the black beans and made limeade. At dinner, I told David our situation, trying to sound calm about the matter.

"Don't worry Mom. Something will break," he said." God won't let us go hungry."

"I hope you're right," I replied. I tossed and turned late into the night, hearing my mother's voice saying she knew we would starve to death in Mexico.

In the morning, I made taquitos, using the last of the eggs and tortillas. I felt like the widow that met Elijah, making the last meal for me and my son. But God had sent help to her, maybe he would do the same for me. At breakfast, I told David to go watch for the mailman. I wanted to ask him about the letters from Texas. He said he would watch. After cleaning the dishes, I went upstairs to pray. I prayed with a fervor which I intended to rattle the walls of heaven, if heaven has walls. I'm sure it rattled something. I wept before the Lord and reminded him of his promises to me and in his word. I told him the world was watching and if he didn't come through they would laugh at me and my God. When David called up, that the mailman had arrived, I ran outside to meet him. I asked if there had been any letters from Texas lately. He replied that he had brought two but when he blew his whistle, I didn't come outside so he took them back to the post office.

"Where are they now?" I inquired in Spanish.

"Possibly at the post office," he replied.

"But you don't know for sure?" I continued.

"No, but that is where I took them. Now I have to go." And with that he left. To avoid theft in Mexico, in the cities, the mailman blows a whistle and if you don't come out, he doesn't leave your mail. They usually bring it back around, but for some reason, he hadn't. The post office was six miles away and the gas gauge in the van, said empty. After thinking about the problem for a while, I knew I had to try to get to the post office. Maybe there was enough gas to get me there. I told David where I was going and climbed in the van and headed downtown. I told myself that the letters would be there, containing cash, because it was virtually impossible for me to get a check cashed. I could buy gas near the post office and go home after stopping at the mercado for food. That was the plan and it seemed simple enough. The gas lasted to within a block of the post office, before the van coughed and died. No problem, I thought, as I steered it to the curb. I could use the can in the back for gas from that station across the street after I picked up the letters. I walked to the post office, fairly confident that all was well. Inside, I explained my situation to the person at the window. She called someone else and I explained again. The postman had returned two of my letters from Texas. They should be there. I wanted them. After forty-five minutes of talking to various people and waiting and talking, it became obvious that the letters were not there. I walked outside, feeling hopeless and angry. I felt that God had let me down. As I walked back to the van, I told God how I felt.

"This is a real mess I'm in God. I am down here trying to do your work and I am depending on you. I have no food, no money, and no gas. I can't even get the van off the street. I guess tonight, the tires and the battery will disappear or the cops will haul the van away." As I was murmuring, I climbed in the van and without thinking, put the key in the ignition and the engine fired. I looked at the gas gauge and it read half full. When it registered what had happened, I began to cry and apologize to God. I was so ashamed of my lack of trust. In Mexico, someone may come and take a little gas from a parked car but they don't put it in! God had sent an angel in my time of need. I cried and rejoiced all the way home.

David's reaction was "wow, really, wow." He had to turn the key to see for himself, for it to soak in. It was too late to go to the orphanage, and when I went to prepare dinner, I remembered there was no food so I made limeade. We still had no money to buy food but I knew God would work it out. In the morning we had only coffee, then David began his school work as usual and I went upstairs to pray. I began to praise and thank God for his goodness and had a good time, worshiping the Lord. Around eleven, David came upstairs to say that a young girl was at the door asking for me. When I went to the door, I didn't recognize her. She said her name was Estella and I had prayed for her mother at a convention downtown. Then I remembered her. Some evangelist from Texas had held a week long revival and somehow heard about me and David. He asked us to come and help pray for the sick after the service. Hundreds usually come through the prayer lines and it takes several people to pray for them all. After I prayed for her mother, Estella had asked for my name and address which I had given to her.

"Come inside please", I said, as I opened the door.

"Thank you," she replied as she entered our bare, little living room. I offered her a paint bucket to sit on and sent David to pick some limes.

"How is your mother?" I inquired

"She is well, and asked me to thank you for your prayers."

"She is quite welcome, but God is the healer and I am always happy to pray for the sick," I replied. David brought in limes folded in the tail of his shirt and dumped them on the counter. He then put ice in the glasses while I squeezed the limes for limeade. I chatted casually with Estella while we were busy, then served the drinks and sat down at the table opposite her, while David settled on a floor cushion.

"My mother sent me to ask you something," said Estella, after taking a drink of the cold limeade.

"What does she want to know?" I asked.

"She wants to know if you could use some furniture. We have some beds and tables in storage."

I was surprised at the offer. Sure, I had been praying for furniture for weeks but perhaps God had misunderstood. What we needed now was food and money. But I simply said it was a gracious offer and certainly, we could use some beds and tables.

"Good," said Estella," when we finish our drinks, if you would take me to my house for the key, we can then go across town to the storehouse for the furniture. My house is not very far."

I agreed to do just that and asked David to go along to help load the furniture. He was eager enough. Estella was about his age and very pretty. Also, he would get to leave his school work for a while. When we arrived at Estella's house, she insisted we come inside and meet her mother. Her mother was a warm, outgoing little woman who hustled about, seeing that we were seated at the dining table. She had lunch prepared and already, two extra plates were on the table. So, God hadn't misunderstood after all. We had a nice lunch of noodle soup, goat's cheese, black beans and tortillas. We shared that welcome meal with Estella, her mother, and a younger sister and brother. After lunch, Estella accompanied us across town, giving directions to the storehouse. We loaded the bunk beds, which were not assembled, and two tables into the van. After dropping Estella at her house, David and I headed home to unload our treasures. When we were alone, I asked David what he thought of the way God had provided lunch for us.

"It was okay," he replied," but I would like to have some meat. I'm not complaining. I would just like to have some meat, that's all." I thought he sounded like an ungrateful Israelite, but said nothing. We unloaded the furniture and carried the bed parts upstairs. As we were putting them together with their various nuts and bolts, we heard a knock on the door downstairs. David ran down to answer and called up that it was Ramon. I stopped my work and went downstairs. Ramon said he and Marta wanted to take us down town for dinner. He said they would pick us up around seven. After he left, I said to David," that was really nice. They have never invited us out to eat before."

"Must be God," was his grinning reply. That evening they picked us up and we went downtown to a very nice restaurant. We were seated at a large family table with Marta and their three teenagers and Ramon, talking, eating and enjoying ourselves, when David looked up from his large plate of beef tacos and said," see Mom, God knew I wanted some meat."

The following day we got a letter in the mail with money inside. Our crisis was over and we hadn't starved after all. We had learned that God was good in a pinch and our faith had grown. The Bible says that trials can build our faith and I know that has been true in my life.

One morning, I awoke with a high fever and a cough. David brought me a cup of coffee and later an apple soda. The following day, David had the same symptoms. I got up and made him some soup and eggs and went back to bed. For the next six days, we had headache, fever and chills and coughed almost constantly. One day, I would try to take care of David and the next day, he would do the same for me. I tried to pray but the fever and headache made it almost impossible to think or concentrate. Finally, I just asked God to send help. Krista came by but didn't stay when she saw we were sick. That same afternoon, Marta came. She had worked as a nurse and was concerned when she discovered us so ill. She said it looked like pneumonia, possibly from a mosquito bite. She went home and got some antibiotics, then returned. She had only enough for one so I insisted that David take them. I thanked God for sending Marta. She came daily and nursed, cooked and cleaned, until after one more week, David was able to get out of bed. A few days later, I followed. It was several weeks more before we were completely well but I would not forget how God sent Marta when I prayed and how compassionately, she had helped us through a terrible ordeal.

After we were on our feet again, a letter came from Kim, saying that she and Jonny were getting married in a month and she wanted us to come home. When I prayed, I felt it was God's will so we began to make preparations to go. Kim wired one hundred dollars for our trip. I remembered that Heidi's flight from Mineral Wells to McAllen cost forty dollars, when Kim graduated. David and I were still, both weak from the pneumonia and he still had a cough. I decided we would take the bus to McAllen, the fare being only six dollars each and then fly to Mineral Wells. I knew it would be much better for us both than the long, tiring bus ride. So the next evening, Ramon and Marta took us to the bus depot where we began, what we thought would be a simple trip home. The only available seat on the bus was the very last row on the aisle. I took it and David put his suitcase in the aisle and sat on it. We had planned to sleep on the bus trip to the border but that was a joke. Each time the wheel hit a pothole, our heads banged against the back of the bus. The noise from the motor beneath us was deafening and the exhaust fumes made us nauseous and aggravated David's cough. It was a miserable night and we both eagerly awaited dawn and arriving at the border. David rustled up some sodas when we arrived, while I waited on the corner with the luggage. After forty-five minutes, the shuttle bus arrived that would carry us across the border. The driver said he didn't stop at the airport but would drop us off as we passed by. When he let us off, my heart sank. We could see the airport about a mile away. We had two heavy suitcases and one overnight bag. We were both sick and weak from the sleepless night on the bus and the only flight for the day was leaving in thirty minutes. I looked at David. He said nothing. I then looked up and said," thank you God for giving us the strength to get there in time." David took two cases, I took the other and we started walking. Before long, some thoughtful soul stopped and carried us to the airport. It was ten minutes until departure time. When I went to the counter to buy tickets, the clerk said," that will be one hundred and twenty dollars."

"I'm sorry," I replied." I thought the tickets were forty dollars."

"They were, until last month. Now they're sixty." After telling the clerk I didn't want the tickets, I went to tell David the bad news.

"What do we do now?" He asked.

"I don't know but we need to eat and then I will think of something, I'm sure." We found a snack bar and had coffee and doughnuts. I felt a bit stronger and counted our remaining funds while we ate, ninety-four dollars and twenty-five cents. I asked David to call the bus depots and check schedules and prices. He said Continental had a bus leaving at eleven a.m. and it was now ten-twenty. The fare was forty-three each. The next bus would not leave until five p.m. We grabbed our luggage and went outside to find a taxi. In our haste to get loaded, the cab driver misunderstood our destination and dropped us in front of Greyhound. I didn't notice the mistake, until he had pulled away. David saw the sign and said," Mom, the Greyhound fare is fifty-two dollars each. We don't have that much money." The cab cost five dollars and he was right. We would barely have coke money after buying the cheaper tickets. It was one more, depressing jolt to our tired minds and bodies. Learning that Continental was six blocks away and having no more fare, we grabbed the bags and half ran, stumbling, crying(me), laughing, to arrive at the depot as the bus pulled in. Hurriedly, I purchased tickets and checked the bags. We found seats and collapsed, exhausted. The air-conditioned bus was freezing to us. We had only light windbreakers and David began to cough. Fourteen hours later, we arrived in Dallas. Kim came to get us at the station. At last, the long, troublesome journey was over. After a nourishing meal and hot shower, we went to bed and slept and slept and slept.

We stayed about a month after the wedding for rest and recuperation. David's cough improved in the hot, Texas sun. I took some odd jobs to earn money for our return trip. The trip back to Tampico was easy and we were both well and strong. The next few months we worked almost daily at the orphanage. We taught the kids about Jesus and shared his love the best we knew how. José Luis accepted Christ as savior, which was a happy moment for us all. Shortly after, it all ended. One day, when we arrived at the orphanage, Magdalena said the Pharaoh wanted us to leave and not return. We were heartbroken. David and I both cried when we hugged the boys and said goodbye. The boys cried, too. I asked Magdalena for a reason but she offered none. Magdalena and supposedly, the Pharaoh were Catholic. I assumed the decision was made when word got around about José

Luis. What I was teaching, was not Catholic. Just Jesus and the Bible, that's all I knew but for me, it was enough.

At home, I began to pray for God's guidance. Should we go back to Texas or stay in Tampico? A few days later, a letter came from Heidi. She and Jerry were getting married in November. Would I come home and help her plan and get ready for the wedding? I felt it was God's answer to my question. It was September, and David's birthday, so Ramon and Marta planned an all day picnic at a beautiful, deserted, beach spot. It would be a birthday party for David and a going away party as well. Their children were there and Hank and Krista and Tammy and a couple of other friends. We had a wonderful day, swimming, exploring, fishing, eating, talking and laughing. At sunset, we headed home and said our sad goodbyes. I wasn't sure if we would be returning to Tampico or not so we packed most of our things into our van and headed home to Texas.

14

When Man's Word Fails

Back home in Texas we moved into the house with my mother temporarily and I took a job as a waitress to help with the bills and Heidi's wedding. I thought Heidi's and Jerry's small church wedding was lovely despite the fact that it rained all day and some gowns and hairdos got wet getting in the church. Another little problem, was the lady who was to decorate the church, was involved in an accident and we had to decorate at the last minute, without her. Heidi's pre-arranged dressing room was locked and no one seem to have the key, which meant she dressed in one tiny room with six bridesmaids and flower girls. Her hair curlers kept getting unplugged, someone moved and lost her makeup kit, the girls stepped on her veil a few times and finally she began to cry and refused to go out of the dressing room. A pep talk from the preacher finally coaxed her out and the wedding began only thirty minutes late.

When I accidentally discovered that some of my family had said they thought that David and I were sponging off Mother, I got upset and moved our few things to our cabin, out on the land. The house was still unfinished. If they had bothered to ask her, they would've learned that I was paying on the utilities and bringing home food. I knew they all disapproved of my move to Mexico but it hurt to know they were saying those things about me. The cabin was fun in the summer but mid-winter was something else. It had no running water and I had to heat and cook with wood but had no wood supply ready. David and I rounded up some deadwood and made a fire. When we went to town for food and supplies, David ran into a friend, who invited him over for the weekend so I let David go. The next day, Friday, I went to work but quit, when my boss yelled at me in front of the customers at the restaurant, for being too slow. He always lost his cool when the place got packed and began to yell at the help. So now,

I had no income and was isolated in my tiny cabin, alone. It was a depressing and sad time. I had no orphanage to work at, no new word from God, no nothing but my own, miserable thoughts. I forced myself to read the Bible in an effort to break the spell of gloom and read in James 1:2 where it says to count it all joy when various trials come upon you and goes on to say that the trying of our faith teaches us patience. I got to thinking about that scripture and decided I had nothing to lose. I would get up and celebrate and count it all joy. I began to sing the song that the Israelites sang after God led them across the Red Sea. Before long, I was dancing around the room and forgetting my troubles." I will sing unto the Lord for he has triumphed gloriously, the horse and the rider thrown into the sea." I was really beginning to have a good time when someone knocked at the cabin door. It was Bill and Maxine Chapman, friends from the church I attended.

"God told us you needed help. He sent us to come get you and take you home with us a few days." I agreed to go and after packing a few things, I left a note for David to come over when he returned. The Chapman's had been attending a large church in Arlington and invited me to go on Sunday. That Sunday was to begin a new chapter in my life. During the service, the pastor announced that there was a visiting missionary in the audience and requested that they stand. Maxine, who was seated next to me, said he meant me.

"Are you sure?" I asked, uncertain.

"Yes, we told him you were with us today." When I stood up, the pastor asked me to come up front, to the microphone.

"I understand you are a missionary to Mexico," he said.

"I was for a while, working in an orphanage but now I'm living in Texas." I was not expecting an interview in front of all those people and it really caught me off guard.

"When are you going back?" He asked.

"I'm not sure, I suppose when the Lord tells me to." I replied

"Well, I want to go on record that when you go, this congregation wants to support your work. How about three hundred a month? Does that sound okay?"

I was appalled." That sounds wonderful," I replied, remembering our limited funds in Tampico." Thank you very much." I'm sure I looked bewildered, because I was.

"Good," he said." Now we have ourselves a missionary to Mexico." He shook my hand and the congregation applauded, loudly. I walked back to my seat, not believing it had really happened.

After the service ended, I was surprised to see a former coworker as she walked up to me. It was Arleta McDaniel and we had both worked for Hydra Rig, an oil field equipment company. I worked in drafting and Arleta was a secretary. She had become a Christian since we worked together. We made plans to get together and soon became friends.

About three months later, on Sunday, a well-dressed couple approached me after church. They introduce themselves as Bob and Betty Carson. They said they heard I was a missionary and I told them that was true. Mr. Carson said he was in the planning stages of an orphanage near Acuña and would like to talk to me about working for him. The Board of Directors was to meet at his home the following week and he invited me to attend. I told him I would come. My old car overheated on the way to the meeting so I arrived a bit late. My first impression of the six, board members was they looked, dressed and acted very socially conscious and upper class, perhaps a bit too much, for my comfort. I kept quiet and listened to the discussion. Bob Carson had sketched a tentative plan for the orphanage building. It was a rectangle, with the kitchen and dining rooms in the center with no light and no outside air. I could smell the grease and smoke from the kitchen, combined with sweaty little bodies and I carefully pointed out what I thought might be a problem.

"I will need something to show the architect in three days," he replied." You used to be a draftsman. Can you draw a plan you think would work, in three days?"

"You write down the basics you want to include, the number of staff and kids you want to accommodate and I will draw it up." I answered.

"Good. Keep up with your hours so we can pay you," he responded.

I said I would and say goodnight. The next two nights, I stayed up into the wee hours, battling a sinus headache, to complete the project. I did a detailed layout of a light, airy and inexpensive edifice built around a garden with tables and benches in the center. I spent a total of sixteen hours on the drawings and delivered them sixty miles to the Carson's house, on the third day. No one was home so I left them at the front door with a note. Much later, I would discover that my plans were stuck inside a closet, unopened. After asking me to do the drawings, Mr. Carson contacted another draftsman, gave him several weeks to do the drawings and paid him a large sum of money for the work. I, incorrectly assumed, that he was using my plans and had just overlooked paying me. I never brought the subject up. That was a mistake that I would later regret. If I had pursued the matter, and learned the truth, I might never have gone to Mexico for Mr. Carson.

He began to call regularly, to talk about the orphanage. He asked if I would go down and take charge of all the details, sort of as a coordinator and later manage the orphanage. It was to be a one hundred unit orphanage and a large project. I told him I would let him know after I talked to David about moving back to Mexico. David agreed to go if he could have a horse or motorcycle so he could get around. Carson invited us both, down on a trip, to see the village where the orphanage would be built. David was on spring break from the Christian school he was attending and I would be free to go. My friend, Arleta, who was developing an interest in Mexico, was also invited to go along with us. We went in a large, luxury van with the Carter's and several of the board members. Bob Carson drove and talked a lot to David on the way down. He said God had just given him a motorcycle and David could have it. He told him how he planned to have a number of horses and cattle at the orphanage and asked David if he would like to be in charge of the animals. He would build a bunk house for David and about three other young men who could help him. David ate it up, hook, line and sinker. Around sundown, we crossed the border at Del Rio. The guards checked us briefly and let us pass. After going through Acuña, we headed east along the border and in thirty minutes, had arrived at the small village of Jimenez, Coahuila. Right outside the village, we reached our destination at a small ranchito. The hacienda was built of adobe, scrap pieces of lumber and tin. It sat, squatting beneath a sprawling mesquite tree. Mama and Papa Mauricio and their son, Ruben, were on the front porch and greeted us warmly as we unloaded from the van.

Mr. Carson had told me and David how God had led him to the elderly Papa Mauricio, who for years had been praying for someone to come and build an orphanage on his land. He had six acres in the heart of the village and over fifty acres, on the outskirts. Mr. Carson had described their meeting as a miracle since he was planning an orphanage. Mama Mauricio served us iced tea with lime as we relaxed and chatted on the porch, in the warm, evening breeze. The single, light bulb, with its audience of moths, cast mystical shadows on the faces of the group. Sitting there in that strange setting, watching the people and the boughs of the mesquite as they swayed gently in the air, I felt as if I was dreaming and that nothing around me was real.

Ruben was tall, muscular and handsome. His voice was gentle, almost soft, which surprised me coming from such a masculine body. He seemed to be in his late thirties. He and David and I were the only bilinguals in the group so we translated for the others. Soon the news of our arrival had spread and the yard became alive with faces of curious friends and neighbors of all ages. Most of them came quietly and smiling up on the porch to meet the Americans and shook our hands. David moved off to the water well with a crowd of young people, conversing noisily in Spanish. They swarmed around him like bees and he loved being the center of attention. Mr. Carson told the Mauricio's that I might be running the orphanage and David would be with me. After visiting for a couple of hours, we went back across the border and stayed in a motel because Mrs. Carson was afraid of Mexico motels.

The next day was spent checking out the proposed building site and meeting the village people. Sunday morning, we said our adioses and headed home. On the trip back, when Mr. Carson asked if I had decided, I asked David.

"What do you think David? Do you want to live in Jimenez?"

"Yeah, Mom, let's do it. I think I would like it."

I told Mr. Carson we would go home and get things ready for the move. He said he would rent us a small house on his next trip down so we could move right away. He also said he would furnish it, pay all expenses and a salary and bring down the motorcycle. It sounded great and I liked the small village and the Mauricio's. I assumed there would be problems because Mexican men are not real big on working with a woman in a management position but with God's help I knew I could handle it.

After going home, Mr. Carson began to call and push me for a moving date. I told him we would go in June after David's school was out. We finally agreed on June 19th. When I asked about the house, he said he hadn't found one yet but promised that he would. We boarded up the cabin, had the electric turned off, and called Mr. Carson on the 18th. His wife said he was out of town on business, had not left any message or money and would not return for a week. That should have been another red flag, but David and I were ready and I couldn't face unpacking and redoing it all so we headed for Jimenez and the Mauricio's. If he had rented us a house as he promised, they would know about it. The trip was long and the highway, virtually deserted in South Texas. One stretch through the woods was so long between service stations, my gas needle hit empty. The doubts and fears began to gnaw at me. What had I done? Everything ahead was uncertain. At home, David had been settled, doing well in school and now here we were in the middle of the wilderness, alone and may run out of gas. If we didn't make it to a station, anything might happen to us on that deserted road. I tried to hide my fear from David and sure enough, over the next hill, a station appeared. I felt the muscles in my back relax as a praise the Lord, escaped my lips.

At dusk, we arrived at the border. We had the usual problems with the Mexican officials, too much stuff. After a long hassle and a little money they finally let me through. It was dark when we pulled into the Mauricio's. They seemed happy to see us but said that Mr. Carson had not rented a house for us. How could anyone be so irresponsible, I wondered. David and I were exhausted and they graciously invited us to stay as their guests until we found a house. We thanked them and went to bed. Tomorrow, I would find a house. In the morning, I awakened to the smell of coffee and eggs. I dressed and went to the kitchen where Mama Mauricio was busy making breakfast. I offered to help but she wouldn't allow it so I asked Mary Ellen, a niece, to show me where to wash up. After grabbing a towel and bar of soap, she led me outside, across the road to a small grove of trees. Inside the grove, was a narrow, shallow, man-made canal, flowing with fresh, cool water from the river. The canal provided irrigation for the small farm and was the summer bathing hole. Mary Ellen left and I sat on the edge of the canal, allowing my feet to dangle in the cool stream while I bathed and brushed my teeth. Listening to the birds and bathing in the river water was quite an invigorating way to begin the day.

At breakfast, the family asked a lot of questions and we answered them. Ruben's brother, Juan, was there. Instinctively, I sensed he was a bitter man and didn't like me or David. To him, David and I were foreigners and out of our proper place. I also knew that Ruben had a warm heart and would be our friend and ally. After breakfast, I left David with Ruben to get better acquainted and I took off in search of a house to rent. Rent houses were scarce in the village and I learned of only two possibilities. The first, was two rooms and no bath. The second, was the former men's clubhouse. It was stucco with one large room and a tiny bath. I opted for the bath, even though there were only half a dozen in the entire village. The floor was tile and I could make cinderblock partitions for our bedrooms. The rent was thirty-five dollars a month. I told the man who showed it to me that I would like to rent it. He said I would have to wait until the next men's meeting, so they could vote on it. That was ten days away. I was disappointed but had learned in Mexico, everything goes slow. When I told the Mauricio's, they insisted we remain at their home and said we would not be imposing. After a week, I went to Acuña and called Bob Carson.

"Well, Jen, I just really haven't had time to find a place for you and David but I will be down in a week or so to get things started." I wanted to say you shouldn't promise what you can't deliver but I held my tongue.

David and I spent the time, waiting to get into our house, by walking around the village and meeting the storekeeper and some of the villagers. We went swimming almost daily in the river and Mary Ellen liked to go with us. She was fourteen and giggled a lot at David, who could be a clown at times. Most everywhere we went, we were watched by the curious. I quickly became tagged as the gringa lady with ojos (eyes) de azul (blue). It seemed to please the people, that we spoke their language and made it easier to become friends. After about two weeks, we moved into our little casa and began to fix it up. I made cinderblock partitions and curtains for the screenless windows. We had one small fan which I perched on top of the cinderblock wall between our bedrooms but it was not enough to keep the mosquitoes off at night. But despite the mosquitoes, and dust from the busy, unpaved street, we soon began to feel at home in our house and in the village. It was a number of weeks before Mr. Carson arrived, and he didn't bring the motorcycle as he said he would. David was disappointed and angry. Once again the man had failed to keep a promise. I began to have serious doubts about our employer. But since we were already relocated, I decided to pray and trust God to take care of things. Carson paid some of the expenses that I had receipts for, but said there was no money for furniture, not even a cook stove or refrigerator. It was just another disappointment, another lie. There was also no money to leave for future expenses. We would make it okay with the three hundred monthly, from the Arlington church but it upset me to have David witness this man's behavior, who called himself a Christian. When he left, he said he wasn't ready to start the orphanage business yet, so I should just continue to get acquainted with the community until he returned.

We continued to visit the Mauricio's a couple of times a week. Ruben was preaching at a week long revival in Piedras Negras and asked if we would come and bring a van load of people from the village, who had no car. I agreed. So, for the next five evenings, we cram packed the old van with an average of fourteen people and went to the meeting. On the second evening, Mama Mauricio had asked us to go to Acuña and pick up her sister and family, so we did. The remainder of the week, David and I loaded up the people in Jimenez, drove thirty miles west, picked up more, back through Jimenez, then thirty odd miles, east to Piedras Negras. Afterwards, we took them all home. It was always after midnight when we got to bed. We were driving one hundred and eighty miles each evening and my van got eight miles to the gallon of gas, but God supplied. Some evenings, I didn't have enough gas money for the trip but one or two of the passengers would offer a little money, never knowing I didn't have it. It was difficult for me to trust God to provide finances, without my help. I was so used to working and paying my own way. I was like the apostles, who after God, had miraculously supplied food for the multitude the third time, were still sweating how they were going to feed the crowd. You would think that after God had sent an angel to put gas in the van in Tampico, I wouldn't have been concerned about gas to carry the people to and from the meeting, but I was. Daily, I would walk and worry and fret and pray and daily God would send his peace and nightly, the gas money would be supplied.

One afternoon, when David and I were outside in our yard, a young man stopped to get acquainted and talk. He invited us to visit the little white church, up on the hill in the village. It was about a mile from our house. I had been praying for God to show us a church to attend, so I told the young man we would visit that evening. It was Sunday and when evening came, we walked to the church and climbed the winding rock steps, that led to the entrance. The sign over the door read," Iglesia de san Juan Bautista". The church was small and freshly whitewashed with a steeple on top. Inside, were fifteen rows of very old, wooden pews, a rather large podium and a communion table with a handmade, lace cloth. Several vases of brightly colored flowers adorned the front of the church. At the door, we were greeted by a short, stout lady with grey hair. She introduced herself as the pastor's wife, saying he was home sick, in bed. Several others, smiled and shook our hands before we took our seats. There was a lot of loud singing, accompanied by guitars and handclapping, then one of the elders read a few scriptures and the service ended with a prayer. After making our way to the front entrance, where I was chatting casually with some of the members, the elder approached and said something rapidly in Spanish, which I didn't understand. I simply smiled and agreed with them, saying "si, si" rather than possibly offending him. He walked away smiling. My bilingual friend, Maria, was there and I thought I would ask her later what he had said but she disappeared. Soon I forgot the matter. At home, David and I agreed we liked the simple, little, white church and the friendly people and decided to make it our place of worship while in Jimenez.

On the following Monday, Mr. Carson arrived unannounced, at our house, with a stranger whom he introduced as chairman of the board of a church that would be providing funds for his orphanage. I had on an old pair of jeans and was doing the laundry in the bathroom. We didn't have a washer or washtub so I put the dishpan in the shower stall to do the laundry. I was hot and sweaty and my hair was a mess when David called out that we had company. I sent David to the store for cold sodas and sat and talked a few minutes with Mr. Carson and his guest. They complimented me on the hominess of our little one-room building with makeshift furniture and no appliances.

"You have really made it into a homey little place, said the stranger." I thanked him but didn't like the way he poked and prodded around the house, picking up David's personal things and nosing around in general. I gave Mr. Carson a report of what we had been doing, provided him with receipts of purchases and ask about the progress of the orphanage plans and the motorcycle. They had come to get things started on the orphanage he said. But he hadn't had time to get insurance for the motorcycle so he had not brought it. David had returned with the drinks and I watched as his shoulders slumped and he dropped his head in disappointment. Saying they were in a hurry and would return later, they left after finishing their drinks.

"Mom, he's never going to bring it, is he? It was all a lie just to get us down here."

"Looks like you might be right David. The man is not very good at keeping his word." That afternoon, as I was preparing dinner, the two men returned. When they came inside, it was obvious that something was very wrong.

"What is it?" I asked." What's wrong?" Mr. Carson stammered a bit as the other man walked back and forth across the floor.

"Jen," began Carson," I'm afraid some things have come up and I'm going to have to dismiss you. You and David need to pack immediately and return to Texas." I felt as if I had been hit in the face with a two by four. David and I exchanged glances. He looked as dumbfounded as I felt.

"What are you talking about?" I asked." What things have come up?"

"Well, Mr. Grayson here, thinks you and David are not the ones for the job here. He doesn't like the fact that you are divorced and wear pants and that David has a Michael Jackson tape. That's not exactly proper for a missionary son." I couldn't believe my ears. I saw the muscles in David's jaw tighten and tears began to run down his face. I took a deep breath and sat down before I fell. After a moment, I replied.

"Maybe your friend should know that I don't wear jeans out in public, that I am divorced because my ex-husband beat us and even tried to kill us and even missionaries sons don't listen to gospel music all the time." I went over to David and put my arms around him. "It's okay," I said, and realized I was crying, too." God will take care of us. He always has. We can find another house."

"That wouldn't be a good idea, Carson said." You need to go back to Texas. We don't want people thinking you represent us any longer."

That stirred the Irish in me. Turning to face him, I spoke slowly and distinctly," Mr. Carson, you don't own me and you don't own Mexico and nobody but God tells me where I can and cannot go!"

"Well", he said." I guess we better go. You can leave the house key at the general store." Then the pair left, rather hurriedly."

David and I talked and discussed the situation, our minds clouded by shock and disbelief. The Bible says we wrestle not against flesh and blood, only the devil, but in the thick of things, it is hard to remember that. We were relieved when bedtime came. Perhaps in the morning, things would look better. Tuesday, I prayed most of the day and felt God wanted us to remain in Jimenez. That evening, I checked on a small, empty house, next door to the medical clinic. It belonged to the county health department and the doctor from the clinic showed me around inside. The bathroom fixtures were broken but Dr. Ricci said we could use one of the two bathrooms at the clinic. It had three rooms and grass in the tiny yard. On Wednesday, Dr. Ricci said the county would allow us to live there and pay only utilities. That was good news and I went home to begin packing.

In the evening when it was time for church, David asked if I was going. I said no because I wanted to finish packing and cleaning and didn't want to stop and get myself ready. So, after he was dressed, he left, saying that he would see me later. When he returned about ten minutes later, and was out of breath, I knew something was wrong.

"Mom," he gasped, catching his breath and continuing," you remember that elder you talked to Sunday on the porch of the church?"

I thought for a moment." Oh yes, the one who talked so fast I couldn't understand him."

"Well, Mom, he was asking if you would preach at the church tonight and you kept saying," si" and they are all waiting on you."

"Oh, dear God, preach in Spanish! I'm not prepared and look at me, I'm filthy! I just can't."

"You have to Mom. They are waiting."

I grabbed a washcloth and haphazardly rubbed some of the grime from my face and arms. Changing clothes in record time, I sprayed on cologne and ran a brush through my hair. I grabbed my Bible and took off in a hurry toward the church, with David. I needed to walk so I could have the few minutes to pray and let God calm me down.

The church was full and the pastor's wife greeted us at the door. She ushered me to the front row of pews and sat beside me. David sat near the back. After the singing was finished, the elder stood and introduced me. When I looked out upon the expectant faces of those forty people, I wasn't as afraid as I thought I would be. Perhaps, if I had had time to think about it, I might have been. Maybe God planned it that way. As I began to speak, the words in Spanish came to me. I spoke on love, how God gives it to us, not to keep but to pass on to others. David smiled and occasionally shook his head in disbelief that I was really doing this. I told the congregation that God's love can bring us peace, healing, food and housing and if we pass it on, that's what it can do for others. At times, the people would clap and say amen or Gloria Dios. A couple of times, they laughed and when I asked, told me the word I had missed. After twenty minutes or so, I had an altar call. To my surprise, two women came for prayer of forgiveness and for healing for their bodies. When it was over, I rejoiced and thanked God. Afterward, virtually every person in church came to shake my hand and offer blessings in Spanish. God had come through. They had listened and received the message. I was dumbfounded that God could use me in such a way. Walking home, David laughed and said," I can't believe you preached in Spanish and they understood you and even responded, my mom the gringa, preacher lady."

Later that week, the pastor of the little church died. David and I went to his funeral. His body was laid on an old wooden bed in an empty store room next to the parsonage. Flowers were hung on the walls. The poor in Mexico, don't use funeral parlors and the bodies are not embalmed, making it necessary to bury them within a few days. It had rained for days and on the day of the burial, his body was carried to the little church. After the service, we walked down the muddy road and up another hill to the cemetery, about a mile away. The pallbearers walked in front, carrying the wooden coffin. The women cried and wailed unashamedly. At the cemetery, the pallbearers sunk deep into the fresh mound of mud, as they lowered the casket into the grave. A few more words were spoken and the crowd watched as scoops of mud were crudely shoveled into the open grave.

Later in the week, the pastor's wife sent a bowl of fruit and requested by messenger, that I come to her house. I accompanied the delivery boy back to the parsonage where she was waiting. After chatting for a few minutes, she asked if I would preach regularly at the church and take her husband's place. Although I had been ordained and sent out by a small church in Texas, I certainly didn't consider myself qualified as a preacher or pastor and told her this. I explained I was only a teacher and servant.

"Teacher, preacher," she replied." What's the difference? You know the word of God and we need to learn it. We need your help."

I told her I would pray and if God allowed, I would try to do the job. She was pleased. When I was certain that God was saying yes, I knew it was no accident that I was in Jimenez when the pastor died. He had a plan all along. I was once again awed at how God has us in his hands. The seeming tragedy with Mr. Carson had become a victory. God was going to use us in Jimenez after all.

15

Adios A Mexico

I continued to teach at the little white church on the hill and God blessed my efforts. The church in Arlington had sent five monthly checks. Most of it was used for helping the needy, food, utilities, gas and repairs for the old van. I had been putting away a small amount each month for a horse for David for Christmas. David had gotten acquainted with Sam and Luisa, the young couple Mr. Carter had acquired to take our place. He brought the motorcycle and gave it to Sam. After a few weeks, it developed a problem and Sam sold it to buy baby food. Mr. Carson hadn't kept his promise is to Sam and Luisa either. After a couple of months they quit and left town. At any rate, I had promised David a horse or motorcycle and intended to see that he got one.

We usually kept clothing and supplies stored in my bedroom and David was always finding needy people and bringing them to the house. One day, he brought a little old man, whose pants were held together on the side with safety pins. David said he never had seen him in any pants but those so he must not have any others. I found him several pants and shirts. He gratefully thanked us in Spanish and went away happy. We had no inkling that the little old man was Pasi's father. Pasi was the village demoniac who walked the streets, sometimes normal but more often, not. He talked to himself and imaginary people, chased away unseen spooks with sticks and although he was harmless, he often behaved in a crazy manner. Pasi had long, matted hair, shirts without buttons, and he held a his baggy pants up with one hand as he ran away from the shameless taunts of village men and children. He would accept cookies at our door but never came inside. David and I prayed regularly for God to help Pasi because we didn't know how to help him ourselves.

In Mexico, the poor, put mentally deficient family members out on the street to beg or scavenge for food. They allow them to sleep inside but put them out each morning until night. After we gave the little man the clothing, I saw Pasi downtown the next day. A crowd had gathered around him and I hurried to him, thinking he might be hurt. Then, I recognized the shirt he was wearing. It was one we gave the little old man. Pasi's hair had been cut and shampooed and he was acting and talking normal. When I asked him about the clothes, he said his papa gave them to him and his mama had cut and washed his hair. The result was astounding. I remember thinking, that's what happens when we share what God gives us with those around us. I hurried home to tell David how God had helped Pasi.

In December, we planned to go to Texas for Christmas and more supplies, when our check arrived from the Arlington church. I told David I had saved for him a horse but we would wait until we returned from Texas, to buy one. He was surprised and happy and agreed that waiting would be best. The check always arrived at our PO Box in Del Rio between the eighteenth and twenty-first day of the month. We packed our bags, and waiting until the twenty-first, went to Del Rio to pick up the check and go home to Texas. But, the check had not arrived. I didn't understand and went to a phone to call the church office. The pastor answered.

"Hello, brother Bill, this is Jen Jireh. I was calling about our support check for this month. It hasn't arrived here."

"Oh, yes, I've been meaning to notify you about that. I had to rent a suite of offices downtown and I'm afraid we have to discontinue your support."

"But I thought it was to be for a minimum of one year," I replied.

"Well, actually it was but the church needs these offices. Ours at the church building are just too small and we can't do both. We're remodeling the sanctuary, too, and that's expensive."

"I see. Thanks anyway. At least now I know why it isn't here. Have a nice Christmas."

"You, too. Bye-bye now," and with that he hung up.

David had been listening and got the gist of the conversation.

"Well, David, they are renting bigger offices and remodeling and there won't be any more support checks."

"Just like that, huh?"

"Just like that," I replied." That means we can't go home. I'm sorry."

"Mom, let's use some of the horse money. I can wait on the horse."

"Are you sure? You have already waited a long time."

"Yes, I'm sure. Do you have it with you?"

"Yes, it's in my purse. Let's fill the van and go home."

"Can we have some tacos for the road?" He asked." I'm starved."

"Sure," I laughed," but don't let Granny hear you say that." He laughed too. We got tacos and headed home to Texas for Christmas. The end of the support checks didn't bother us a lot. By now we had learned to accept that man will fail you, but God will not. On our trip home, in our tired but blessed, old van we talked and laughed and looked forward to Christmas with the family.

At home, we spent a happy and refreshing two weeks. When we visited the Arlington church they had collected a load of clothing and supplies for us to take back to Mexico. One couple asked if we could get a sofa across the border for our house. When I thought of our cold, hard, metal folding chairs, I said we could try. After services, we followed them to their house and picked up a cherry colored sofa and chair from their garage. They fit in the van with the food and clothing but it was so packed out, I wondered if we would find space for our suitcases. The van had windows all along the sides and in the back door. I knew the border guards would want a fifty dollar bribe if they saw the sofa. I began to pray for wisdom to get the load across without paying fifty dollars. The devil knew I didn't mind the loading or hauling or the long tiring trips but I hated the border crossing with a passion. He sat on my shoulder and kept saying," you'll never get it across the border, never, never, never!" I just kept telling him that God would make a way where there seems to be no way and God would help me get that beautiful, wonderful sofa across.

A few days later, we squeezed our luggage in with the load along with a bag of food to eat on the road and started south. The nearer we got to the border the harder I prayed. I had timed the trip so we would be crossing at night. Sometimes, the guards were half asleep. In Del Rio, I had a brainstorm. Stopping at a market, I bought a box of aluminum foil and David and I covered the back windows with it. Then I put our luggage behind the seat and covered it with a blanket. The guard would not be able to see anything but the front seat. Then I headed to the border, praying in the spirit rather vigorously. It was around midnight, and sure enough the single guard was dozing. When we pulled up, he walked toward us rubbing his eyes.

"What is your destination?" He asked.

"Jimenez," I replied.

"Okay, go ahead." As we pulled out, I watched in the side mirror. When he headed back to his chair, he suddenly became awake. Seeing the foil covered windows, he turned and began running after the van, waving his hands in the air.

"David, he's chasing us!"

"Goose it Mom, and get around the corner. He won't catch us," was David's wise reply. That is precisely what I did and we trucked it on home watching over our shoulder for a flashing light, the remaining thirty miles.

In the spring, David located a quarter horse at a ranch near town. It was wild and unbroken and cost three hundred dollars. I had only two hundred and fifty and David liked the horse so the rancher said that we could pay the fifty later. We bought it. It was a handsome, young stud named Tonka and the caballeros were afraid to go near him but David got three ropes around his neck. With two men on horses and David walking, they got him to pasture near our house, which we rented for five dollars a month. Later in the week, I noticed that Tonka kept losing the oats out of the side of his mouth when he tried to eat. David brought his friend over who knew horses and he said we had been taken. Someone had broken Tonka's jaw while trying to break him. He would never feel the rein on that side and would always have a problem eating. I went to talk to the rancher but he refused to return our money. But generously, I thought, offered to drop the remaining fifty dollars. In spite of the handicap, David broke Tonka and taught him to eat out of his hand. He became extremely gentle. The local cowboys began to take note of the young man who tamed the wildest horse in the area.

One day while praying, I began to feel an urgency to pray for Heidi. I prayed, but that feeling that something was wrong wouldn't leave me. I kept praying and told David on Friday, we were going to Del Rio to call home. Something was wrong with Heidi. I didn't understand it, because we had a friend in Del Rio with a phone who had agreed to bring us emergency messages but none had come. There was only one phone in Jimenez and it was in the new, men's club and wasn't available for public use. On Friday, we packed a bag, just in case we had to go home and went to Del Rio. There, we learned when we called, that Heidi had been hospitalized for days in critical condition but was improving. Being four months pregnant, she went on a long-awaited ski vacation with her husband and several friends to Colorado. Her appendix had ruptured and caused a lot of pain but she kept quiet because she didn't want to spoil the trip. Eventually, she went to the lodge doctor who said she had a ruptured appendix and immediately sent her to Denver, by ambulance. The doctors there suggested immediate surgery but Heidi wanted to fly home to Fort Worth for the surgery. After she signed a release that they would not be held responsible if she died enroute, the doctors reluctantly allowed her to go. An ambulance was waiting in Fort Worth at the airport where she was transported to the hospital. Miraculously, she didn't lose the baby, and the organs near the appendix had formed a pocket, not allowing the poison to spread. We went to Texas and Heidi was soon well enough to leave the hospital. The family had tried to call the emergency number in Del Rio but the eighty year old grandmother, who was hard of hearing, answered and hadn't understood the message.

When we returned to Jimenez in a couple of weeks, a lot of bad things had happened. The rancher, where we had left Tonka, said the horse had died while we were gone. Whether it was true or not, we would never know, for he said he was too busy to take David to the carcass. We were heartbroken. The pro-Communist Party won the local election and made us move out of the house that belonged to the county. The place we moved into, had no windows and doors as it had never been finished. I had doors put in but couldn't afford windows as it was a big house. The wind, dust and rain were constant problems. We had dirt floors where the tile had never been laid. I got a terrible throat infection and was not able to swallow. The high fever made me delirious and I thought I might die. Dr.Ricci was out of town and when David went for the only other doctor, she refused to come to our house and I couldn't get out of bed. David did his best to care for me and after a couple of weeks, God healed me.

I was grateful to the kids and others who sent money when God allowed, but I felt it was time to go home. I needed a long rest and recuperation. I was bone tired, weak and burned out. The people came daily to the door with needs and I went and prayed and chauffeured and helped and taught and gave, but there seemed to be precious little of me left to give. I sought God and he allowed us to return to Texas. Leaving, as always, was very sad. We loved the little village, the people, the church and the work but it was time.

16

Reflections

The house in Mineral Wells is finished now. Thanks be to God and to all who helped but mainly, Paul. Sometimes, I sit out on the porch, early in the morning, drinking coffee and watching the sun come up as the birds and squirrels begin to stir. I think about my life and the choices I made.

The children are all grown and married now, learning and growing in the Lord. David graduated from a technical school in the Metroplex last year and is working there as a computer, designer-drafter. Kim and Jonny live in South Carolina with their two children. Kim took nurses training and works in a hospital and Jonny is still in the Marine Corps. Paul is married and lives in Mineral Wells with his wife and son and daughter. He works as a welder for an oil company. Heidi and Jerry have three sons and live at a small community about ten miles down the road. Heidi is a nurse and Jerry has a cabinet shop. Mother is over eighty and lives in Mineral Wells. I visit her regularly and we occasionally play her favorite game of cards, Skip-Bo. She usually wins. I travel around the county teaching four-year-olds for Head Start and make an occasional trip to Mexico with a few other missionaries. I know one day, I will once again live on the mission field and do God's work. I have a vision of a mission in Baja, Mexico and am currently praying about it. I never met Mr. Right but it has long since been a priority in my life. But who knows, God's timing is perfect.

I think about how God has answered many of the questions I asked when I first began this journey. Is God real and alive today? Most definitely. He's proved it a thousand times in a thousand different ways. Did he come to earth and hang on the cross for us? Without a doubt. He loved us and it was the only way. Can anyone find Jesus? Yes, by sincerely asking him to make himself known to you. He revealed himself to me and the Bible says he is no respecter of persons.

Finding him is not what makes you a Christian. You must believe he is the son of God, confess and repent of former sins and begin to follow him. Is the Bible true and inspired of God? Every word of it. I have tested it, tried it and seen the devil flee too many times to recount, when I have resisted him, quoting the word of God, as Jesus did. He doesn't expect us to make it alone. We begin to read his word and live it with his help. How does one follow, with so many, teaching and preaching so many different messages? The Bible says for every man to work out his own salvation with fear and trembling and that's what we should do. Stay in God's word, pray daily and ask the Holy Spirit to lead you. Is there a baptism of the Holy Spirit and unlearned languages? Yes, it is in the Bible, a part of the New Testament church and if it has passed away, how can I and countless thousands of others have it today? It gives me power to be and do whatever God asks. Are miracles for real and still happening today? Unquestionably. I have witnessed and experienced hundreds of them. How do we glorify God, as the Bible teaches we are to do? I believe that his instruction manual, the Holy Bible, teaches that we (1) accept Jesus and allow him to become Lord and master of our lives, (2) endeavor daily to become more like him by reading and practicing the word and following his examples and by praying,(3) allow his love and his spirit to make us lights and witnesses to our families, our communities and our world. Jesus testified constantly of God and so should we.

As Christians, we socialize and congregate largely with other Christians. As a result, we sometimes hurt each other and sin against one another. It is inevitable, but God can't use us if we harbor unforgiveness. For me, this has been one of the most difficult things to do in following Jesus. To forgive a brother or sister who has intentionally or otherwise caused serious hurt to me or my children. To achieve it, I have to stay humble before the Lord and daily repent of things I might have said or done or left undone that hurt others. If we are sincere in asking, he will show us our mistakes and is quick to forgive us when we repent. I ask God to make me willing to forgive others, as usually I cannot do it on my own. Soon he will heal the hurt and I forgive the offender. The unlovely incidents, recorded in this book, come not from bitterness or unforgiveness but were included because they were important events that tended to shape the lives of me and my children.

Is it easy to follow Jesus and walk in the spirit? No, not always. Jesus says in Luke 9:23," "if any man will be my disciple, let him deny himself and take up his cross daily and follow me." It is never easy to deny the flesh for growth in spirit.

Is it worth the effort? I have staked my life on the belief that it is. I was walking on Pensacola Beach one day, thinking that it was sometimes hard to be a real Christian, when God spoke to me and said," pick up a grain of sand." I thought it was a strange request but nevertheless, reached down and got some sand on the end of my finger. With some difficulty, I finally isolated a single grain. God spoke again and said," that grain of sand is this present life. The beach, for as far as your eye can see, is eternity with me. Would you not willingly exchange one grain for the entire beach?"

I'm the first to admit that with all my experiences, I'm no super saint, far from it. I get upset, confused, afraid, angry and bullheaded at times but never for long. I believe and trust the Lord with my whole heart and he has gently pulled me away from my worldly desires and onto a path that leads to eternity with him. I desire to help others find the straight and narrow path and experience his reality and his love. There have been and will be times of pain, hardship and suffering, along with the peace and joy as long as we live on this present earth. If it is God's will, I am ready and willing to die for his sake. I will never deny him or his word, for being close to him at times, I have caught a glimpse of what is waiting on the other side and felt the joy of being with him. I will never again try to make my own path or go my own way. I will always seek and try to follow a better way, the way he chose.

The end.

If you have questions or prayer requests, contact Jennifer at P.O. Box 342, Santo, Texas 76472